Anatomy of No Contact

SURVIVING SILENCE & RECLAIMING YOUR INNER POWER

SAGE CHARIE MONROE

Copyright

Epigraph

When you let go of what no longer serves you,
you make space for what truly matters in your own life.

Dedication

To those who chose themselves when it was the hardest choice to make, this book is for you. May you find strength in your silence, power in your healing, and the courage to always choose and love yourself.

Preface

This book is written to explore the emotional journey of choosing no contact when a relationship ends. It is a journey that often begins with confusion, heartbreak, and pain, leaving the person who was left behind wondering why it ended. For some, it might feel like being disregarded, thrust into a spiral of self-blame, anger, or heartbreak. Whether the relationship lasted days, weeks, years, or decades, once a connection forms, it leaves a profound emotional impression.

Through this book, Kellie's story offers readers an intimate look into the turmoil of her breakup with Rob. Rob's decision to abruptly walk away from their relationship left Kellie in emotional chaos. While Kellie had sensed Rob's push-and-pull behavior and the instability it brought to their connection, she had already fallen deeply in love with him. Like many, she was caught in the cycle of emotional triggers that kept her tied to the relationship despite the roller coaster it had become.

Kellie's story takes readers through her raw and honest journey of processing her pain. Through her daily journaling, reflections, and moments of vulnerability, she sheds light on what it feels like to choose no contact and silence as a means of self-preservation. Her story highlights the challenges of not reaching out, the heartache of letting go, and the deep emotional wounds that come with healing.

This book explores the reality that choosing yourself is rarely easy. It requires confronting pain head-on, sitting with discomfort, and finding the strength to move forward. But Kellie's story also reveals how silence and distance can create the space for profound growth, self-love, and transformation.

For anyone who has endured the heartbreak of a relationship's end, this book will resonate deeply. It is a testament to the power of reclaiming your inner strength, even when it feels impossible, and to the ultimate reward of choosing self-love in the face of loss.

Contents

1. ANATOMY OF NO CONTACT   1

2. A Journey of Healing and Self-Rediscovery   2

3. Introduction   3

4. Part I: Anatomy of No Contact   6

5. The Day of the Breakup   7

6. Choosing No Contact   10

7. Kellie's Post Break-Up Journal Entries   13

8. Journal Entry—Day 1: Mood—Sorrowful & Over-whelmed   14

9. Journal Entry—Day 2: Mood—Heavy, Emotional   18

10. Journal Entry—Day 3: Mood—Confusion and Anger.   22

11. Journal Entry—Day 4: Mood—Restless, Conflicted   26

12. Journal Entry—Day 5: Mood—Restless, Anxious   29

13. Journal Entry—Day 6: Mood—Exhausted, Slightly   34
    Hopeful

14. Journal Entry Day 7: Mood - Triggered, Disempowered   39

15. Journal Entry—Day 8: Mood—Hurt, Awakened, De-   45
    termined.

16. Journal Entry—Day 9: Mood Determined, Conflicted,   49
    Vulnerable

17. Journal Entry—Day 10: Mood—Guilt and Self-Re-   53
    flection

18. Journal Entry—Day 11: Mood—Heavy, Conflicted,   59
    Resilient

19. Journal Entry—Day 12: Mood—Reflective and   65
    poignant, tinged with vulnerability and a sense of
    self-discovery.

20. Journal Entry—Day 13: Mood—Emotional exhaus-   71
    tion, mixed with a hint of emerging clarity and resolve.

21. Journal Entry—Day 14: Mood—Tentative Resilience,   75
    Mixed with Determination and Pain

22. Journal Entry Day 15: mood - mix of longing, pain, and 78
    a sense of resignation

23. Journal Entry—Day 16: Mood—conflicted, vulnera-   83
    ble, and anguished, with a subtle undercurrent of grow-
    ing awareness.

24. Journal Entry—Day 17: Mood— introspective, melan-   88
    cholic, and conflicted, with an undercurrent of
    self-awareness and painful realization.

25. Journal Entry Day 18: Mood~Hopeful Yet, Cautiously   95
     optimistic, With Undercurrents of Tension And Un-
     ease

26. Journal Entry—Day 19: Mood—oscillates between de-   100
     spair and hope, underscoring the complexity of navigat-
     ing heartbreak and personal growth.

27. Journal Entry—Day 20: Mood—hopeful and intro-   104
     spective, tinged with a sense of determination.

28. Journal Entry—Day 21: Mood—resilient and intro-   108
     spective with undertones of determination and self-em-
     powerment.

29. Journal Entry Day 22: Mood~Resilient and Introspec-   112
     tive with Understones of Determiantion and Self-em-
     powerment.

30. Journal Entry—Day 23: Mood—hopeful and deter-   115
     mined.

31. Journal Entry—Day 24: Mood—determined and   118
     hopeful, with an underlying sense of empowerment and
     self-awareness.

32. Journal Entry Day 25: Mood ~ Reflective and Resolute,   122
     with undertones of Emotional Pain and Growing Em-
     powerment.

33. Journal Entry Day 26: Mood~Hopeful and Empow-   126
     ered, with an Undertone of Reflection and Guarded
     Vulnerability.

34. Journal Entry—Day 27: Mood—reflective, empow-   130
     ered, and content.

35. Journal Entry—Day 28: Mood—conflicted yet intro-   134
     spective, evolving toward empowerment and gratitude.

36. Journal Entry—Day 29: Mood—calm, resilient, and   139
     self-assured, with an undercurrent of gratitude and
     self-awareness.

37. Journal Entry—Day 30: Mood—lighthearted, carefree,   144
     and rejuvenated.

38. Journal Entry Day 31: Mood~Conflicted and Intro-   148
     spective, with a Strong Undercurrent of Anxiety and
     Disempowerment.

39. Journal Entry—Day 32: Mood—a combination of   153
     self-awareness, determination, and resolve, tempered by
     a lingering sense of frustration and regret over past
     choices.

40. Journal Entry—Day 33: Mood—optimistic, empow-   159
     ered, and resolute.

41. Journal Entry—Day 34: Mood—joyful, confident, and   163
     accomplished.

42. Journal Entry—Day 35: Mood—hopeful, reflective,   167
     and anticipatory.

43. Journal Entry—Day 36: Mood—empowered, reflec-   170
     tive, and indifferent.

44. Journal Entry—Day 37: Mood—reflective and em-   175
     powered, with a mix of detachment and self-awareness.

45. Part 2: Anatomy of No Contact   179

46. Journal Entry—Day 38: Mood—contemplative and   180
     conflicted, with an undertone of cautious resolve.

47. Journal Entry—Day 39: Mood—reflective, resolute,   184
    and empowered.

48. Journal Entry Day 40: Mood~Reflective, Resolute, and   188
    More Empowered.

49. Journal Entry Day 41: Mood~A Combination of De-   191
    termination, Empowerment, and Self-Awareness.

50. Journal Entry—Day 42: Mood—reflective and res-   195
    olute, with undertones of lingering sadness and self-em-
    powerment.

51. Journal Entry—Day 43: Mood—uplifted, reflective,   199
    and self-affirming.

52. Journal Entry—Day 44: Mood—a blend of introspec-   203
    tion, determination, and triumph.

53. Journal Entry—Day 45: Mood—reflective and opti-   208
    mistic.

54. Journal Entry—Day 46: Mood—reflective, empow-   212
    ered, and hopeful, with an undercurrent of melancholy.

55. Journal Entry—Day 47: Mood—a mix of excitement,   217
    gratitude, and disbelief, coupled with a touch of nervous
    anticipation.

56. Journal Entry—Day 48: Mood—a blend of anxiety,   222
    self-doubt, and introspection, but also includes an un-
    dercurrent of determination and a desire for self-em-
    powerment.

57. Journal Entry—Day 49: Mood—amazement and   226
    pride; empowerment and transformation.

58. Journal Entry—Day 50: Mood— a mix of empowerment, pride, and introspection with moments of temptation and resolve.   231

59. Journal Entry—Day 51: Mood—a mix of empowerment, pride, and resilience.   236

60. Journal Entry—Day 52: Mood—empowered, introspective, and resolute.   241

61. Journal Entry—Day 53: Mood—calm, reflective, and empowered.   244

62. Fast Forward Six Months Later: I Chose Myself, and That Changed Everything   248

63. Final Post Break Up Journal Entry   252

64. Epilogue   255

65. FAREWELL   258

66. About the Author   260

67. Chapter 67   262

ANATOMY OF NO CONTACT

Surviving Silence and Reclaiming Your Inner Power

A Journey of Healing and Self-Rediscovery

The hardest battles yield the greatest transformations.

-Sage Charie Monroe

Introduction

No Contact isn't just a rule—it's a rebellion. A severing. A last, desperate act of self-preservation when love has become a slow erosion of the soul. It's the moment you realize you're standing at the edge of an emotional abyss, and the only way to survive is to walk away—not because you want to, but because staying would mean losing yourself entirely.

It means no more texts sent into the void, hoping for a reply that will never come. No more scrolling through their social media, dissecting every post for hidden meaning. No more rationalizing the way they pulled away, the way they made you feel small, the way they kept you just close enough to keep you hoping.

No Contact is the excruciating decision to stop begging for breadcrumbs, to stop arguing with ghosts, to stop trying to resurrect something that was already dead. It is sitting in the wreckage of a love that once felt invincible and making the brutal choice to stop searching for the pieces. Because the truth is, the pieces are not yours to gather. They never were.

And so, the silence begins.

This book is an intimate, unfiltered descent into that silence—the unbearable, deafening void left in the wake of heartbreak. Through Kellie's journal entries, we witness the raw unraveling of a woman who gave everything, only to be left with nothing. She is stripped bare, grappling with the echoes of a love that once defined her, now reduced to unanswered messages and cold memories.

The Anatomy of Heartbreak: Breaking and Becoming

At first, the silence is torture. Kellie fights against it, filling the space with doubt, longing, rage. She replays every conversation, searching for the moment it all fell apart. She questions herself—Was I too much? Not enough? Should I have stayed quiet, settled for less, swallowed my truth just to keep him?

But No Contact is not just an absence; it is a reckoning.

The withdrawal is brutal. Her body betrays her—sleepless nights, an ache lodged deep in her chest, a hollow hunger that food cannot fill. Her mind torments her—memories flood in uninvited, regrets claw at her resolve. Every instinct screams for her to reach out, to make it make sense, to force closure from a man who has already made his choice.

And yet, through the chaos, something begins to shift.

This book is divided into two parts: The Destruction and the Rebirth

Part One: Surviving Silence – the battle with emptiness, the unraveling of self, the excruciating process of detaching from a love that once felt like oxygen.

Part Two: Reclaiming Inner Power – the quiet awakening, the slow rebuilding, the moment Kellie stops mourning the past and starts choosing herself.

Each journal entry is followed by an analysis—a dissection of the emotional turmoil, the psychological patterns, the subconscious wounds that No Contact forces to the surface. We break down what it means to let go, to stop seeking validation, to confront the demons that made her cling to a love that was never truly safe.

This is not just a story of heartbreak—it's a survival guide for the soul. A roadmap for anyone who has ever lost themselves in the arms of another, only to wake up one day and realize they were never held at all.

No Contact is not about punishment. It is not about winning or proving a point. It is about saving yourself from the slow decay of self-betrayal.

And in that silence, there is something unexpected—power.

The power to heal.

The power to rise.

The power to never again beg for a love that should have been freely given.

Part I: Anatomy of No Contact

Surviving Silence

The Day of the Breakup

The silence after the last message wasn't empty—it was suffocating. A void so vast it swallowed me whole. It wasn't just the absence of his words; it was the absence of everything I had known—love, certainty, the illusion of safety. No contact wasn't a decision. It was abandonment, a cruel echo of something that once was, now reduced to nothing.

I should have seen it coming. The signs were there, whispering in the quiet spaces between us. The last time we sat together, he ordered pizza, his voice hollow, his touch distant. The air between us had thickened, suffocating, filled with something unspoken but undeniable. I knew then—long before the words were said—that I was already losing him.

And then, on July 4th, the message came, shattering the last fragile piece of hope I had left:

"Happy 4th of July. I hope you're having a good day. I've decided to take some time off and contemplate us."

The world tilted. Take some time off? The words blurred, twisted into something unrecognizable. I read them over and over, searching for a different meaning, but there was none. He was leaving. Slipping through my fingers like sand, dissolving into the space between us as if I had imagined him all along.

Panic erupted inside me, frantic and uncontrollable. My hands shook as I typed, my mind a storm of confusion and fury. *What is happening*? *What changed*? *We need to talk. How could you do this to me*? I sent message after message, desperate for something—an explanation, a reason, a lifeline. My heart pounded in my chest, erratic, screaming for a response.

But nothing came.

The silence wasn't just quiet—it was final.

I stared at my phone, waiting, praying, pleading with the universe to make it buzz. Seconds turned into minutes, minutes into hours, and still... nothing. The night stretched on, long and merciless, shadows clawing at the walls, pressing in around me.

And then it hit me—he wasn't coming back.

The urge to send one more message was almost unbearable. My mind raced with all the things I could say, all the ways I could make him feel what I was feeling. Anger burned at the edges of my grief. I wanted to lash out, to shatter the silence with my pain. But deep down, in the hollow space where hope used to live, I knew the truth.

It wouldn't change anything.

No contact wasn't a strategy. It was the wreckage left behind after a storm. It was the only thing I had left. This wasn't about dignity or strength—it was about survival.

I had spent so long trying to hold onto something that was never really mine. I had lost myself in him, in the weight of his absence, in the desperate need for his validation. And now, all that was left was me, standing at the edge of something dark and unfamiliar.

The silence stretched on, endless and unforgiving.

And for the first time, I let it.

Choosing No Contact

W hat happens when the silence doesn't break? When you're left alone with nothing but the echoes of a voice that no longer reaches for you? When every familiar routine is suddenly foreign, and the absence of their presence is so loud it drowns out everything else? How do you find yourself when the person who once felt like home is now just a ghost in your memories? How do you rebuild a life when the foundation you stood on has crumbled beneath you?

It all seems impossible.

No Contact is more than just avoiding texts, calls, or accidental run-ins. It is a severing, a self-imposed exile from something that once felt vital. It is choosing to walk through the fire of loneliness rather than grasp at the dying embers of what was. It is about reclaiming yourself from the wreckage, but before that can happen, it is about enduring the storm of withdrawal.

The process is brutal. It does not unfold neatly, nor does it adhere to a predictable timeline. No Contact is not a singular decision, but a battle fought in small, agonizing moments—when your fingers hover

over their name, when nostalgia threatens to rewrite history, when you question if leaving the door open would hurt less than bolting it shut. The mind, desperate for comfort, clings to illusions of what could have been, while the heart aches under the weight of unfinished conversations and unsaid goodbyes.

This journey unfolds in stages, each with its own torment and transformation. The following sections delve into these phases as Kellie journals her raw emotions, unraveling the depths of heartbreak, confusion, and self-reckoning.

Dissecting the Pain: Anatomy of No Contact

Beyond the emotional waves, The Anatomy suggests a meticulous and almost surgical exploration of the no-contact process—dissecting it layer by layer, piece by piece. The term anatomy itself evokes precision, an unflinching examination of what lies beneath the surface. It is a postmortem of a love lost, an autopsy of longing, an investigation into the wounds that refuse to heal.

No Contact is not just a rule—it is a psychological and emotional upheaval that rewires the brain and body. This section does not merely describe the stages; it delves into the visceral, internal experience of severance. It examines:

The Mind's Rebellion – how logic and longing battle for dominance, how denial morphs into desperate justifications, how silence triggers the brain's craving for dopamine-fueled interactions.

The Body's Withdrawal – the physical manifestations of grief: the tightness in the chest, the sleepless nights, the hollow ache in the stomach that no food can fill.

The Emotional Warzone – the pendulum swing between nostalgia and anger, between yearning and resentment, between wanting them back and wanting to erase them altogether.

This section unearths the psychological warfare that unfolds within—how the need for closure becomes a mirage, how self-worth is tested, and how, despite it all, survival is possible.

Ultimately, The Anatomy serves as more than just an analysis—it is a revelation. It is a roadmap through the abyss, guiding readers not just to understand their pain but to transcend it. No Contact is not simply about removing someone else; it is about reclaiming yourself. It is about stepping into the silence and, rather than waiting for it to break, learning to find your own voice within it.

Kellie's Post Break-Up Journal Entries

Journal Entry—Day 1: Mood—Sorrowful & Overwhelmed

T he words spill from me, messy and unfiltered, as the pain crashes over me in waves so fierce I can hardly breathe. It's unbearable. I close my eyes, and suddenly, I'm back there—the night we met, beneath a blue moon that hung high in the August sky, casting its glow over everything. Rob arrived on his Harley, and without hesitation, I climbed onto the back, my arms wrapped around his waist, the roar of the engine vibrating through me. It felt like the start of something electrifying.

We rode to a local bar, where the hum of a live band blended with our laughter. The attraction was instant, undeniable—a spark that caught fire in an instant. Conversation flowed effortlessly, our words weaving a connection that felt both new and familiar. When it was time to part, we lingered, eyes locked, the night thick with the unspoken. I remember thinking, this could be something real.

By morning, a text lit up my phone. *Good morning, beautiful*. And just like that, a rhythm began—messages that stretched through the day, checking in, sharing moments, building anticipation. A few days later, he invited me over for dinner.

That night, Rob cooked for me. He poured me a glass of wine, his own drink an Old-Fashioned, his favorite. We slipped into the jacuzzi under the moonlight, steam curling around us like whispers. The air was thick with laughter, teasing, and something deeper—something unspoken but felt. The warmth of the water, the way his eyes held mine—it felt like the beginning of forever.

But tonight, forever feels like a lie.

The memories hit me like a punch to the chest. One moment, I'm fine; the next, tears spill down my cheeks, unstoppable. It hurts—God, it hurts—to accept that it's over. That I can replay every second, but I can't bring it back to life. That no matter how much I miss him, no matter how many times I reach for my phone, the reality remains the same.

Today, the weight of it all feels unbearable. The sadness, the longing, the frustration—it's all tangled together, pressing down on me. I want to reach out. I want to hear his voice, to close the gap between us, to undo whatever went wrong. But deep down, I know—I know it won't change anything. And yet, the urge is there, strong and relentless.

So, I write.

Because the words are too heavy to keep inside. Because my mind won't stop questioning—Was I not enough? Did I mean so little?

I realize now how much of myself I tied to him. Not just for love, but for a sense of stability, a sense of home. And without him, everything feels off-kilter, like I'm standing on unsteady ground.

I don't have answers. I don't have closure. But I have this moment. And for now, that has to be enough.

So, I'll sit with the pain. I'll let it move through me, rather than bury it. I'll take this one breath, one hour, one day at a time.

And somehow, someday, I'll get through this.

Reflection & Analysis: The Ache of Loving & Letting Go

Kellie's mood, as expressed in her journal entry, is a complex mix of emotions. She feels emotionally inundated, describing her pain as unbearable and noting that her emotions are "the weight of it all is unbearable." The central tone of her writing reflects profound sadness and grief over the loss of her relationship with Rob.

Kellie reminisces about the romantic and joyful moments of their relationship, amplifying her sense of loss. She grapples with unanswered questions and a lack of closure, questioning her actions and worth in the relationship. Choosing silence, while intellectually understood, leaves her feeling helpless and isolated, intensifying her frustration. Without Rob's presence and the connection, they shared, she feels off-balance and as though she is missing. Amidst heaviness, there's a subtle current of resilience and hope as she resolves to take things one day at a time and allow herself to heal.

Kellie begins by expressing the raw intensity of her emotions: "the pain crashes over me in waves so fierce I can barely breathe." This vividly conveys how deeply she feels the loss, setting the tone for the entry. The weight of her heartbreak is palpable, and her struggle to process it highlights the overwhelming nature of grief when love ends. Her tears and feelings symbolize the emotional disorientation common in the aftermath of a meaningful relationship. She recalls the enchanted beginning of her relationship with Rob, describing their first meeting under a blue moon and their shared adventures. The details—the Harley ride, the live band, and their shared chemistry—paint a picture of an idyllic romance. These memories, cherished as they are, also intensify her pain, as they serve as reminders of what she feels she has lost. This juxtaposition between the bliss of the past and the emptiness of the present is central to her turmoil.

Kellie acknowledges her reliance on Rob for comfort and stability, reflecting on how his presence became a foundational part of her life. This recognition is significant as it suggests that her pain is not only about losing Rob but also about losing the sense of security and identity she derived from their relationship. Her questions— "Was I not enough? Did I mean so little?"—reveal an internal struggle to reconcile her self-worth with the breakup.

Amidst her despair, Kellie expresses a glimmer of hope. By writing down her feelings, she demonstrates a proactive step toward processing her emotions. Her commitment to taking things "one day at a time" and allowing herself to feel underscored by her resilience. She recognizes the importance of honoring her emotions as part of her healing journey.

Journal Entry—Day 2: Mood—Heavy, Emotional

Today, a tidal wave of raw sorrow crashed over me, ripping the air from my lungs before I could even brace myself. I was drowning in the acrid taste of my own tears, each one a burning reminder of us—every stolen laugh, every whispered secret, every heartbeat we once shared. I longed to freeze time, to clutch those fleeting, tender moments in my hands, but time is a ruthless predator, devouring memories and leaving nothing but an echo in its wake.

The silence now is a relentless torment. I stare at my phone, my eyes burning as I search for a flicker—a single vibration or a name lighting up the screen—that might bring him back. Instead, I'm met with an endless void, a gaping absence where his presence once lived. My mind loops, dissecting every word, every pause, every lie. Was I too much to ask for? Did I misread the love we shared, or was I merely a convenient placeholder until I wasn't needed anymore? In my desperation, I sent him a trembling text: "This silence is hurting me. I care about you; I need to know what changed." But my words vanished into the void, swallowed by nothingness.

Rob was never one to bare his soul. He was always there, yet always out of reach—a phantom drifting through my life on a highway of adventure: ski trips, mountain bike rides, cross-country escapes—while I remained here, marooned in the wreckage of what might have been, endlessly waiting for his return, for a scrap of his attention, for a promise he never meant to keep. Now, I'm left questioning: was I ever truly part of his world, or just a fleeting stop on his endless journey?

The weight of it all is a crushing pressure on my chest—a constant, gnawing ache that steals my breath. I write because the storm inside me is too fierce to contain. I spill these raw words onto paper, hoping that each syllable might chip away a little of the crushing burden. Perhaps, one day, this relentless sorrow will finally loosen its grip, leaving only scars in its wake.

Until then, I drag myself forward, breath by trembling breath. Even as my heart shatters with every beat, I cling to the desperate hope that I am not completely broken—that this overwhelming pain, as vast and consuming as it feels now, will not be the end of me.

Reflection & Analysis: The Overpowering Wave of Grief

Kellie's journal entry is a searing, visceral plunge into the depths of heartbreak, capturing the raw torment of longing and the relentless ache of loss. Her words are drenched in imagery and metaphor, painting a picture of overwhelming sorrow that is almost tangible. Kellie describes her pain as a "tidal wave of raw sorrow" that crashes over her, ripping the air from her lungs. This metaphor not only conveys the intensity of her emotions but also suggests that her grief is all-encompassing and suffocating. It's as if every part of her body is under siege by the relentless force of her memories.

The description of drowning in the "acrid taste of my own tears" is both disturbing and deeply evocative. Each tear is not just a drop of water but a burning reminder of every shared laugh, whispered secret, and heartbeat they once enjoyed. Kellie's fixation on her phone—staring, searching for a sign of his return—speaks volumes about how his absence has transformed her world. His memory permeates every moment, turning even the most mundane aspects of life into painful reminders of what's been lost. The void on her screen becomes a symbol of the emptiness that now dominates her existence.

The internal dialogue—questions like "Was I too much to ask for? Did I misread the love we shared?"—reveals her deep-seated self-doubt. This is not just mourning a lost relationship; it's a brutal self-assessment that leaves her feeling diminished and unworthy, as if she were merely a convenient placeholder. Her desperate text—"This silence is hurting me. I care about you. I need to know what change d."—is a cry for closure that vanishes into nothingness. This moment encapsulates the agony of unreciprocated effort. She reaches out, hoping for an explanation, but instead, her words are swallowed by the relentless silence.

Kellie contrasts Rob's elusive nature with the tangible presence of her own suffering. While he drifts through life on endless adventures—ski trips, mountain bike rides, cross-country escapes—she remains anchored in the wreckage of their failed connection, wondering if she was ever truly part of his world. Despite the crushing weight of her grief, Kellie turns to writing as a means to exorcise her pain. The act of spilling her raw emotions onto paper is portrayed as a small, yet significant, rebellion against the darkness that surrounds her. Each word is a step towards reclaiming herself, even if only a little at a time.

The closing lines, where she clings to a desperate hope that she is "not completely broken," underscore the enduring resilience within her. Even as her heart shatters with every beat, there is a stubborn determination to survive, to move forward "breath by trembling breath." It's an admission that the path to healing is slow and uncertain, but that the fight is still worth it.

Journal Entry—Day 3: Mood—Confusion and Anger.

Three days without him, and I'm caught in an unrelenting storm—a maelstrom of raw, jagged grief that leaves me gasping for air. I stare at my phone, desperate for a flicker of his presence, but there's only silence—a void that mocks every word we once shared. The sting of his absence, of his indifference, cuts deeper than any cruel remark, leaving me to wonder if I ever truly knew him at all.

After a year of shared moments—dating, texting, entwining our lives—I'm left with nothing but echoes. I want to scream, to lash out with furious texts that tear at the fabric of my hurt: "How could you just ignore me? How could you discard every memory we built?" But the words freeze on my lips, swallowed by the same silence that now defines us.

I should have trusted my instincts when his signals grew murky, when his warmth became a cold game of push and pull. Time and again, he vanished into the shadows of uncertainty—one moment igniting my heart with attention, the next leaving me stranded in a bitter void. I clung to the hope that this would be just another phase, that if I held on long enough, he would choose me. I was wrong. I was addicted to his sporadic affection, a moth drawn to a flame that scorched me every time I reached out.

I remember his words from our early days—a promise of something real. Even after a month, when he hesitantly confessed, "I've enjoyed our time together, but I don't think we're the match I was looking for," I held onto the memory of his return. He would always come back, and in those moments, I believed I was his entire world. His texts were my lifeline, each one a fragile promise that buoyed my heart through the day. Without them, anxiety creeps in, and I feel lost, untethered, aching for that familiar connection.

Somewhere along the way, I began to measure my worth by the rhythm of his messages. I was once confident—a woman who thrived on her own passions and joys—but now, my identity blurs into his presence. I hung on every update about his day, every mundane detail he shared, as if they held the key to my validation. Slowly, I surrendered pieces of myself, convinced that his fleeting attention was worth sacrificing my own happiness.

The relentless fear of losing him gnaws at me, an ever-present shadow that forces me to cling to every interaction, every text—a desperate attempt to stave off the emptiness. And now I know, with a clarity that cuts through my soul, that this fear was never just about Rob. It was about losing the part of me that believed I was enough on my own, the part of me that had been buried beneath a mountain of his indifference.

In the end, the absence of his voice, his touch, his reassurance leaves me questioning not just our past, but who I have become—a hollow shell desperate for validation in a world that no longer echoes his name.

Reflection & Analysis: The Haunting Void

Kellie's journal entry is a searing portrait of heartbreak—raw, unfiltered, and unyielding in its portrayal of loss and longing. Her words capture a moment where absence becomes a tangible weight, a relentless presence that suffocates every trace of hope.

Kellie's opening lines plunge us into a world where Rob's absence haunts every corner. The metaphor of a tidal wave ripping the air from her lungs isn't just poetic—it's visceral. It underscores how his silence isn't merely an empty space; it's a force that actively crushes her spirit. Her fixation on her phone, the desperate search for any sign of him, shows how deeply his presence was once interwoven with her daily existence. The void that now replaces his voice transforms every mundane moment into a stark reminder of what has been lost.

She describes how each memory-every laugh, whispered secret, and shared heartbeat—plays over and over in her mind like an old film reel. This continuous replay is both a comfort and a torment, locking her into a cycle of nostalgia and regret. Kellie's internal questions—wondering if she was too much, or merely a convenient placeholder—reveal how her self-worth has become entangled with his attention. It's a painful self-scrutiny that leaves her feeling diminished, as if the more she revisits the past, the less of herself she finds in the present.

Kellie acknowledges how the highs of their connection once made her feel whole, even euphoric. Rob's intermittent affection was like a lifeline that buoyed her through the day, yet its absence now leaves her adrift and unmoored. This push and pull, the unpredictable oscillation between connection and abandonment, has eroded her confidence and slowly blurred her sense of self. The journal entry reveals the raw paradox of longing for someone who not only failed to nurture her but also warped her internal gauge of worth.

The entry is suffused with self-doubt and introspection. Kellie's questioning—whether she misread the signals, whether she was too much—acts as a harsh internal verdict on her own value. There is a palpable sense of betrayal in not just the loss of the relationship, but in the realization that she had come to measure her happiness by the sporadic rhythm of his texts. The relentless fear of being replaced, of being forgotten, leaves her grappling with the painful notion that she might not be enough on her own.

Yet even as Kellie's words drown in despair, there's an undercurrent of defiance. Her admission that she writes to chip away at the burden of sorrow is a quiet act of rebellion against the all-consuming pain. Each word on the page is a small reclaiming of her agency—a promise that despite the relentless ache, she is still fighting to rebuild herself, one trembling breath at a time.

Journal Entry—Day 4: Mood—Restless, Conflicted

I found myself staring blankly at my phone, its screen a blur from my tired eyes, desperate for a message from Rob—anything to break the silence. Every fiber of me ached for even a single word, a whisper of what we once shared. I felt an irresistible pull to reach out, to scroll through his social media, to dissect every conversation until I was convinced I had missed a hidden sign or that I could have done something differently.

Yet, somewhere in the depths of my despair, I clung to the last fragile piece of self-respect. I kept reminding myself: if Rob truly cared, he would have reached out. He had chosen to end it all. His silence was his final act. As much as a part of me yearned to chase him, I knew deep down that doing so would only strip me of what little dignity remained.

It stings to accept that if he never bothered to check in, why should I force myself into the emptiness of his world? That thought, as painful as it is, serves as a stark reminder: I deserve more than crumbs—a love that chooses me fully, without hesitation or second thoughts.

Even now, the urge to call him is overwhelming, a magnetic force pulling at my heart. But I know that giving in will only deepen my sorrow. So I hold on, clinging to that tiny shard of self-respect, one trembling moment, one desperate urge at a time, determined to reclaim my own worth from the wreckage of our past.

Reflection & Analysis: The Battle Within

Kellie's journal entry is a raw, unflinching exploration of the pain of longing and the battle between dependency and self-respect. In her words, we witness a powerful tug-of-war: on one hand, the deep, aching desire to reach out to Rob—a need to fill the void his absence has left—and on the other, a stubborn, rising insistence that she deserves more than his intermittent crumbs of affection.

Kellie's confession, "Every part of me wanted to hear from him... trying to figure out if I missed something," lays bare her desperate need for connection. It's not just about missing a person; it's about clinging to the remnants of a love that once made her feel whole. The repetitive replays of their past conversations reveal a mind ensnared by unresolved questions—each replay deepening her sense of loss and confusion.

Her inner dialogue is a testament to the war waged inside her. When she reminds herself, "if Rob had wanted to reach out, he would have," it's a moment of painful clarity—a rational attempt to break free from the magnetic pull of his absence. Yet, the constant sting of silence makes that truth nearly impossible to accept. Kellie's words capture this heartbreaking paradox: despite the logic telling her to let go, every fiber of her being still yearns for his attention.

A crucial turning point in her reflection is the realization that she deserves more than "breadcrumbs of attention." This is where Kellie begins to reclaim her identity, even as she grapples with the deep-seated wounds left by his inconsistent love. The awareness that she no longer wants to base her self-worth on Rob's fleeting validation is both liberating and excruciatingly painful. Her decision not to reach out—despite the overwhelming urge—marks a courageous, if tentative, step toward emotional independence.

Her closing promise, "I'll get through this—one moment, one urge at a time," is a fragile beacon of hope amid the storm. It acknowledges that healing is not immediate or linear but a gradual process of reclaiming control, piece by piece. Kellie's self-awareness shines through as she vows to resist the toxic cycle of dependency and instead nurture her own worth.

Journal Entry—Day 5: Mood—Restless, Anxious

L ately, sleep has become a stranger. My nights are restless, haunted by dreams that twist into nightmares, leaving me breathless in the dark. My mind loops endlessly, retracing every word, every moment, trying to pinpoint the exact place where it all unraveled. I wonder—was it my fault? If I had swallowed my need for certainty, if I had let the days drift by without asking the hard questions, would he still be here? I keep thinking that if I had not mentioned the future, if I had just gone along with things and avoided those difficult conversations, things would have been different. But deep down, I know I wanted clarity. I needed answers to ease the doubts I felt about the relationship. But deep down, I know the truth. I wasn't asking for too much. I was asking for honesty.

Rob. Charismatic, self-assured, effortlessly handsome. His silver-streaked hair and the rugged elegance of his beard carry the weight of experience, of stories untold. He walks with the ease of a man who knows who he is, and I was drawn to that certainty, to the quiet confidence that made the world seem a little more steady when he was near. He is the first man I've dated who is a decade older, and I found his maturity intoxicating—a glimpse into a life fully lived, wisdom etched into the fine lines around his blue eyes.I once teased him about being a playboy, a joke laced with the kind of curiosity I wasn't ready to name. But the way he bristled, the way his defenses snapped into place, caught me off guard. "Accusatory," he called it. I wasn't sure what unsettled me more—his reaction or the feeling that, somehow, I had touched a nerve he didn't want exposed.

The truth is, for all the confidence I wear like armor, I felt small around him. I could hold my own in charm and wit, and I knew I was beautiful in my own right, but standing beside his success, I found myself second-guessing everything I had built. My career, my ambitions—they were solid, yet they felt like pebbles beside his mountains. Without realizing it, I let his validation become the mirror in which I measured my own worth.

Looking back, I see it clearly now—I didn't just fall for Rob; I fell for the idea of him, for what he represented. I became so wrapped up in his world, his presence, his approval, that I forgot the weight of my own. I lost sight of the fact that I, too, brought something rare and beautiful to the table—kindness, integrity, depth. But somewhere along the way, I let my insecurities whisper lies, convincing me I wasn't enough.

And that is what I regret the most. Not losing him, but losing myself in the process. I made myself smaller to fit into the space he allowed, afraid that standing fully in my light would push him away.

But love—real love—should never require me to shrink. It should never ask me to be less than I am.

So I am learning. Learning to stand tall again, to reclaim the parts of myself I tucked away for the sake of someone else's comfort. Because the love I deserve is one that sees all of me and does not flinch.

Reflection & Analysis: Yearning & Uncertainty

Kellie's initial thoughts, a tendency to internalize the failure of the relationship: "I keep thinking that if I had not mentioned the future, if I had just gone along with things and avoided those difficult conversations, things would have been different." This self-blame reflects her struggle to make sense of the breakup, despite knowing deep down that her desire for clarity was valid.

Kellie's admiration for Rob's confidence, "I was drawn to that certainty, to the quiet confidence that made the world seem a little more steady when he was near," highlights the magnetic pull Rob had over her. However, this admiration with Rob was coupled with insecurity about Kellie's own accomplishments, leading her to feel small in comparison. Her reflection— "I became so wrapped up in his world, his presence, his approval, that I forgot the weight of my own," shows how her insecurities caused her to prioritize his validation over her own sense of self-worth. This imbalance made her feel diminished, despite recognizing her own positive qualities.

As Kellie reflects on the relationship, she begins to identify where things went wrong—not just externally but within herself: "My career, my ambitions—they were solid, yet they felt like pebbles beside his mountains. Without realizing it, I let his validation become the mirror in which I measured my own worth." Her acknowledgment of this pattern is a crucial step toward healing and growth.

Kellie's description of how she placed Rob on a pedestal illustrates the imbalance in their dynamic. While Rob's success and charisma captivated her, they also became a source of comparison, leaving her feeling inadequate. Kellie's admission that Rob's validation became the measure of her self-worth, reveals how she lost her sense of autonomy in the relationship.

By tying her self-esteem to Rob's approval, she unintentionally reinforced her insecurities. Her insecurity led her to feel small in the relationship, suppressing her own strengths and achievements to avoid conflict or risk losing Rob. This self-diminishment contributed to her feelings of inadequacy and imbalance in the relationship.

Kellie's realization that "Because the love I deserve is one that sees all of me and does not flinch," underscores the importance of authenticity in relationships. A healthy partnership should nurture both individuals' strengths rather than amplify insecurities. Kellie's reflection on her qualities— "kindness, integrity, and depth"—shows a growing appreciation for what she brings to a relationship. This acknowledgment is a step toward rebuilding her confidence and self-worth.

By admitting that, "I didn't just fall for Rob, I fell for the idea of him, for what he represented," Kellie takes accountability for her role in the relationship dynamic. This self-awareness empowers her to make different choices moving forward. Her statement— "So I am learning. Learning to stand tall again, to reclaim the parts of myself I tucked away for the sake of someone else's comfort"—signals a shift in her mindset. She is beginning to recognize that true love supports rather than undermines her sense of self.

The incident where Rob reacted defensively to Kellie's joke about being a "playboy" highlights the fragility of their communication. His overreaction suggests unresolved insecurities, while Kellie's surprise shows a lack of emotional safety in their interactions. Kellie's insecurity and Rob's perceived confidence created an uneven dynamic where she felt the need to prove her worth, sacrificing her own emotional needs in the process.

Journal Entry—Day 6: Mood—Exhausted, Slightly Hopeful

Today, I am a body, not a person. Just a shell, a hollowed-out thing moving through time without meaning. I haven't showered in days—what's the point? My skin feels foreign, as if it doesn't belong to me. The smell of stale sheets clings to me. My stomach is knotted so tightly I can barely swallow water, let alone food.

I wake up gasping for air, like I've surfaced from drowning, but I never actually make it to shore. I just keep sinking, deeper, deeper, into a place where the pain is everywhere. It sits on my chest, it claws at my throat, it makes my limbs feel too heavy to move.

And today, I think about a different kind of pain.

Something sharp. Something external. Something I can control. Because this ache inside me is too vast, too relentless. Maybe if I could just make it physical, I could contain it. Maybe then I could breathe again.

But instead, I make a different choice.

I don't know why. Maybe out of desperation, maybe because I don't trust myself alone with this feeling. Maybe because even the wreckage of me still wants to survive.

I drag myself to the yoga studio. My limbs resist. My grief resists.

It tells me: Stay in bed. Rot here. You belong to me now.

But I go anyway.

The moment my bare feet touch the mat, I almost collapse. I don't belong here. I don't belong anywhere. But the instructor tells us to breathe, so I do. Deep, shaky, reluctant.

And then I move.

It's mechanical at first—a body obeying commands, not a person seeking peace. I fold, I stretch, I hold poses that should feel grounding but instead feel foreign. My muscles tremble. My mind screams.

But something happens.

For just a moment, the pain quiets.

I inhale. Hold. Exhale.

And suddenly, I am no longer drowning.

The grief is still there, but it is in the background now, distant, like an echo instead of a scream. My body moves through the poses, and for the first time in weeks, I feel something other than emptiness.

It doesn't fix me. Nothing can.

But for the first time, I wonder if I might survive this.

I made dinner when I got home. A small thing—just eggs, toast, something to put in my body so I don't disappear completely.

I sit at the kitchen table, chewing slowly, like I'm relearning how to be a person. The food tastes like nothing, but I swallow anyway. That has to count for something.

That night, I lie in bed, staring at the ceiling, waiting for the usual war inside my head to start.

The war comes, but it's quieter this time.

I still wake up reaching for him.

I still feel the ache settle against my ribs, heavy and cruel.

I still mourn.

But I also breathe.

And for the first time, sleep finds me before the grief does.

This pain isn't going anywhere. It still owns me, still whispers to me, still wants me to stay broken.

But somewhere inside me, something stirs.

A flicker. A whisper. A maybe.

Maybe if I keep moving, if I keep breathing, if I keep showing up for myself—maybe I will make it out of this.

Maybe one day, the pain won't feel like a living thing inside me.

Maybe one day, I will wake up and not feel like I'm suffocating.

Maybe one day, I will exist beyond this grief.

Maybe—just maybe—I am not meant to stay broken.

Reflection & Analysis: Drowning in the Aftermath

Kellie's journal entry is visceral—a raw portrayal of grief as something that takes over the body, the mind, and the will to exist. This isn't just heartbreak—it's a complete unraveling of self. The depth of despair here is suffocating, yet within it, there is a flicker of defiance—a refusal to fully surrender to the void.

Kellie is not speaking from a place of clarity or closure—she is inside the storm, inside the ache that feels like it will never loosen its grip. She is drowning, but she is also clawing for air. The entry begins in a place of complete physical and emotional collapse. "I have not showered in

days, barely eaten anything, and my stomach is constantly in knots."
This is not just sadness; this is full-body grief. The kind that renders
basic human functions—eating, sleeping, even moving—nearly impossible. It's not just an emotion; it's a state of being. "I caught myself
thinking about another type of pain just to cope—something physical
to distract me from this emotional storm inside me."

This is one of the most hauntingly honest lines in the entry. The
emotional pain is so unbearable that the idea of physical pain becomes
a relief. This is not necessarily self-destruction—it is the desperate
search for something tangible, something she can understand, something she can control. This is where grief turns dangerous. When
suffering becomes so overwhelming that any form of escape feels like
salvation. It is a breaking point.

And yet, Kellie does something extraordinary. "But today, I made a
small decision that felt huge: I forced myself to go to the yoga studio."
The choice to move—to leave the suffocating space of grief—is a small
rebellion against despair. It is not a cure, not a grand transformation,
but it is an act of defiance. Her body wants to stay in bed. Her mind
wants to drown in sorrow. But she moves anyway. "It did not fix
everything, but for the first time in a while, I noticed my breathing
slowing down."

This is the first moment of relief. Not happiness, not healing—just
a small shift. The pain is still there, but for a fleeting moment, it is not
the only thing she feels.

This is significant. Not because yoga changes her life, but because
it reminds her that something else exists beyond the pain.

Kellie struggles of relearning how to live, "When I got home, I made
myself dinner—a simple meal, but it felt like an achievement." This
moment is so powerful in its quietness. It is the realization that healing

is not just about big victories—it is about survival in the smallest of ways:

Eating when you don't feel like eating.

Sleeping when you don't feel like sleeping.

Moving when you want to stay still.

These are the victories that grief does not want you to have.

This is not joy. It is not relief. It is not even hope. But it is momentum.

One of the most profound elements of this entry is the absence of resolution.

"The pain will not disappear overnight." "The grief still owns me, still whispers to me, still wants me to stay broken." Unlike many stories of healing that end in revelation, this one doesn't. Kellie does not emerge victorious. She does not suddenly feel free. She does not claim to be over him. But she does not surrender.

The Flicker of Something Else: The Maybe

"Maybe one day, the pain will just be a scar, instead of an open wound."

"Maybe one day, I will wake up and not feel like I'm suffocating."

The word "maybe" is crucial here. It is not a declaration of healing. It is not a promise that everything will be okay. But it is the first sign that she is willing to believe in a world beyond this pain. The fact that she moved her body means she is still fighting. The fact that she ate means she is still choosing to exist. The fact that she wrote this entry means she is still searching for meaning.

Kellie is still in the storm. She is still lost. She is still grieving. But she is also breathing, moving, trying. This entry is not about healing—it is about surviving. And sometimes, survival is the bravest thing you can do.

Journal Entry Day 7: Mood – Triggered, Disempowered

Today is worse. So much worse.

It feels like the universe itself is mocking me, weaving Rob into everything I see, everything I hear, everything I breathe. His ghost lingers in the spaces between seconds, in the pauses of my day, in the moments where silence used to be filled with his voice.

The songs on my playlist? Ruined.

The streets I drive down? Laced with memories.

The time of day when he used to check in? Now a slow, agonizing realization that he won't.

Everywhere, everywhere, everywhere—it's all him.

We shared four seasons together. How do you forget someone after that? How do you erase the feeling of watching the leaves turn while holding his hand, that first night where he pulled me close, the summer nights when we whispered under the stars, the spring mornings when waking up next to him felt like a promise?

You don't.

And that's the torture.

It's only been a week since we last spoke, but it feels like eternity has stretched itself around my longing, trapping me in a loop of replaying everything that led to this.

And with each replay, I feel smaller. Weaker. More disempowered.

Did he ever really love me? Was I just a placeholder, a brief amusement, a temporary fix for his loneliness?

I should have seen it coming. The signs were there—the pull, the push, the dizzying dance of affection and withdrawal. The way he would pull me in so deeply, make me feel like I was his world, and then—without warning—disappear into the void.

I should have known it wasn't real.

But I wanted to believe it was.

And now, I feel sick with the realization that maybe it never was.

I am angry. At him, at myself, at the universe for bringing me to this place where I feel so raw, so ruined.

Because I know—I KNOW—what a real man does. A real man does not make the woman he loves question where she stands. He does not keep her guessing, does not throw her crumbs of affection only to starve her of reassurance.

A real man makes her feel safe, not anxious.

A real man does not let her go to sleep questioning her worth.

A real man does not put himself in the position to lose her.

And Rob? He let me go so easily. Like I was nothing. Like I was replaceable. Like I didn't matter.

And that realization cuts deeper than any cruel word he could have said.

I know now—Rob was never my forever.

But knowing doesn't make it hurt any less.

Knowing doesn't erase the way my body still aches for his presence, the way my soul still reaches for him in the middle of the night. Knowing doesn't erase the desperate, clawing need to hear his voice just one more time, to rewrite the ending, to make him see what he's lost.

I know walking away is right. I know staying would only mean losing myself.

But right now?

Right now, I don't want to be strong.

Right now, I just want him.

Even if he's wrong for me.

Even if he never really loved me the way I loved him.

Even if it destroys me.

Reflection & Analysis: A Love That Refuses to Let Go

Kellie's journal entry is a brutal, unflinching descent into the depths of heartbreak—an intimate, visceral look at what it means to grieve someone who is still alive, someone who chose to leave. The emotional landscape here is not just sadness; it is a labyrinth of longing, self-doubt, fury, and unwilling clarity.

This is not the kind of pain that fades quietly. This is the kind that burns, lingers, and carves itself into the marrow. What makes this entry so devastatingly immersive and painfully real is how it captures the contradiction of loss—the knowing and the wanting, the clarity and the craving, the awareness that leaving is necessary but still aching for the very thing that is breaking her. This is not just heartbreak; this is withdrawal.

Kellie's journal begins with a relentless sense of entrapment. "It feels like the universe itself is mocking me, weaving Rob into everything I see, everything I hear, everything I breathe." This sets the tone for inescapable grief—not just the loss of Rob, but the way his presence lingers in places where he no longer exists.

The world itself feels like a cruel reminder, as if it refuses to let her forget. "His ghost lingers in the spaces between seconds." This isn't just about missing someone—it's about being haunted by them. His absence is not just a void; it's an active presence, a shadow stretching over everything. "Everywhere, everywhere, everywhere—it's all him."

The repetition here is suffocating, mirroring the obsessive nature of grief. This is what heartbreak does—it turns the mundane into landmines. Every song, every street, every small moment becomes a portal back to what once was. This passage masterfully captures the way a person can become a world—and how, when they leave, that world turns into a prison.

One Week Without Rob: The Disempowerment of Replaying the Past

Kellie is trapped in a loop, replaying their relationship, searching for answers that will never come. "With each replay, I feel smaller. Weaker. More disempowered." This is where the self-doubt starts creeping in. Heartbreak is not just about losing someone—it's about losing yourself in the process. The more she relives it, the more she questions her own reality. "Did he ever really love me? Was I just a placeholder?" The pain of being replaceable, of being temporary, of being convenient is one of the cruelest parts of this kind of loss. Rob's actions left her in a state of uncertainty, and now she is searching for proof that she meant something.

"I should have seen it coming." Here comes the self-blame, the dangerous notion that she should have been able to protect herself from this. But love—especially toxic love—thrives in the space between reality and illusion. He gave her just enough hope to stay, just enough love to make her doubt his indifference. This section is the darkest part of the grieving process—the place where she begins to turn the knife on herself.

Anger Beneath the Ache is the war between love and rage. Kellie's anger is a defense mechanism, but it is also an awakening. "A real man does not make the woman he loves question where she stands." This is the moment of clarity—the understanding that love should never feel like this. That love is not supposed to be a guessing game, a puzzle, a punishment. "And Rob? He let me go so easily. Like I was nothing. Like I was replaceable."

The shift here is devastating. This is the realization that she was always more invested than he was. That while she was making him her world, he was keeping his options open. "And that realization cuts deeper than any cruel word he could have said." This is where the true grief lives. Not in the fact that he left, but in how effortlessly he did it. Because when someone leaves easily, it forces you to wonder if they ever truly cared at all. This section is rage-filled, but it is also empowering. The anger is what will eventually save her—but not yet.

Clarity is a Double-Edged Sword: Knowing What's Right & Wanting What's Wrong. This is the most tragic part of the entry—because awareness does not equal healing. "I know now—Rob was never my forever." This is the hardest truth to accept. It is not that she doesn't know what's right—it's that knowing doesn't stop the pain. "Knowing doesn't erase the way my body still aches for his presence." This line is devastating because it captures the brutal contradiction of heartbreak.

The mind knows, but the body remembers. The hands still crave his touch, the lips still anticipate his kiss, the soul still reaches for him in the dark. "Right now, I don't want to be strong. Right now, I just want him." This is rock bottom. This is the battle between self-worth and addiction. Because Rob wasn't just a person—he was a drug. And even when she knows he's toxic, the withdrawal is unbearable.

"Even if it destroys me." This is not just longing. This is the collapse of self-preservation. The willingness to trade self-worth for one more moment in the illusion.

This is love at its most dangerous.

Kellie's journal entry is not about moving on—it is about the war before that. The war between: Clarity and craving; rage and longing; knowing what's right and wanting what's wrong.

This is where heartbreak is the most dangerous—when you are aware of the toxicity but still shackled to the need for them.

Because anyone who has ever ached for someone who was bad for them knows this feeling—the feeling of knowing you should walk away, but still hoping they'll turn around.

This is not closure. This is not healing. This is the moment before the fight to let go truly begins. And this moment?

It is the most excruciating of them all.

Journal Entry—Day 8: Mood—Hurt, Awakened, Determined.

The silence today was unbearable. My mind raced with endless thoughts, trying to understand why Rob ended things the way he did. Could he have been cheating? Found someone else? Or, worse, was I just a side piece all along? The possibilities made my heart ache with pain and deceit, and my mind spiraled into places too dark to bear.

The silence gnawed at me. It felt like a punishment I could not escape, so I reached for my phone, desperate for relief, and sent Rob a message: "This silence is hurting me in the process. I care about you. I wish you can communicate how you feel."

I did my best to keep it composed, not letting my emotions spill over. But I waited...and waited. No reply. Nothing. And in that moment, I confronted the harsh reality of being ghosted. The pain was unlike anything I imagined—intense, raw, and overwhelming.

Then, a realization hit me like a wave. How did I allow myself to tolerate such disrespect from a man? Why was I so ready to sacrifice my peace just to hold on to him? I began to question myself, and painful truths surfaced—Am I drawn to partners who manipulate and control? Is this pain rooted in something deeper—abandonment wounds from my past? Have I been giving my power away in relationships without realizing it?

This reflection shook me to the core. I realized that this pattern might have been ingrained in me, but I am not defined by it. I do not want to live my life dependent on others for validation. I cannot allow my sense of worth to be dictated by someone else's treatment of me.

Today, I set a new goal for myself: I will do whatever it takes to make emotional progress. I am choosing to focus on my well-being, to take control of my life, and to stop being a victim of circumstance. I deserve peace, freedom, and happiness, and I am the only one responsible for creating it.

Rob's silence gave me a harsh but necessary message: I can't rely on others to fill the gaps within me. From this point forward, I am taking charge of my life. I am reclaiming my power. I refuse to allow anyone—especially someone who disrespects me—to dictate my worth.

This is the start of something new. It won't be easy, but I know I have the strength to see it through. I will not allow myself to be hurt like this again. My happiness is my responsibility. No one else can take that away from me.

Reflections & Analysis: Reclaiming My Worth from the Echoes of Absence

The silence Kellie experiences is devastating: "The silence gnawed at me. It felt like a punishment I could not escape." This highlights her longing for closure and validation from Rob, which intensifies the emotional void left by his absence. Kellie's introspection leads her to question her patterns in relationships: "Am I drawn to partners who manipulate and control? Is this pain rooted in something deeper—abandonment wounds from my past?" This acknowledgment is a critical step toward understanding the underlying issues that may have contributed to her vulnerability.

Despite her initial pain, Kellie finds strength in confronting harsh truths: "I realized that this pattern might have been ingrained in me, but I am not defined by it." She shifts her focus from external validation to self-empowerment, resolving to take control of her emotional well-being. Kellie's decision to prioritize her happiness and stop tolerating disrespect marks a significant shift in her mindset: "I refuse to allow anyone—especially someone who disrespects me—to dictate my worth."

While Rob's silence is painful, it also serves as a wake-up call for Kellie to reevaluate her self-worth and dependence on others. This forced introspection propels her toward self-discovery and healing. By acknowledging her potential patterns of seeking validation or gravitating toward controlling partners, Kellie demonstrates emotional maturity and a willingness to break free from destructive cycles. Kellie's realization that "My happiness is my responsibility" is empowering. This shift in perspective allows her to reclaim agency over her life and emotions, marking a departure from victimhood.

The intensity of Kellie's pain underscores the depth of her emotional investment in the relationship. However, her ability to channel this pain into motivation for change reflects her resilience and determination. Kellie does not shy away from the pain she feels; instead, she allows herself to confront it head-on. This willingness to face discomfort is a sign of emotional strength and a critical step in the healing process. By recognizing the potential roots of her emotional wounds, Kellie is taking ownership of her healing journey. This self-awareness will be instrumental in helping her establish healthier boundaries and relationships in the future.

Kellie's resolution to "make emotional progress" demonstrates her commitment to personal growth. This focus on self-improvement will help her build a stronger sense of self-worth and resilience. Kellie's decision to "stop being a victim of circumstance" signifies a powerful shift in her mindset. By taking control of her narrative, she is reclaiming her power and redefining her path forward.

Journal Entry—Day 9: Mood Determined, Conflicted, Vulnerable

I woke up today determined to focus on myself. It was time to heal, seek help, and regain my emotional strength. I reached out to my therapist and opened up about the relationship struggles that had been weighing me down. Talking about it gave me a sliver of hope—hope that things could get better, that I would find my footing again.

When I got home, I noticed a shift in my thoughts. I realized that I can only control myself and my mind—not what goes on in Rob's. Whether he had moved on, found someone new, or had emotionally checked out long before our breakup, those thoughts were tormenting me, and I had to let them go.

I decided I needed to replace the old with something new. I would try new activities, explore hobbies, and fill my cup with things that nourish me. For the first time in days, my mind felt a little more at peace.

Then the phone rang...

I looked down at the caller ID: Rob. My heart skipped a beat, and I froze. I was not sure whether to answer. I knew I was not ready for any conversation with him yet. I left the phone ringing and sent it to voicemail.

When I saw the voicemail notification, I felt a strange mix of relief and dread. Should I listen to it? What would he say? Would he confess that he had found someone else? Offer friendship? Explain why he left? A part of me did not want to know.

I listened anyway. His voice sounded calm and composed—so unaffected by everything I had been through.

"Hello, Kellie. This is Rob. I hope that you are having a fun weekend. I'm heading over to my buddy's house to help him move things in his garage and thought we should talk after. It is getting harder to do this as time goes on."

He sounded detached—like the past week had meant nothing to him. All the emotional spiraling I went through...and here he was, casually suggesting we talk. He did not even seem to realize the emotional impact his actions had on me.

I sat there, confused, and afraid. Do I even want to know why he broke up with me? What if it was something I couldn't bear to hear? I realized I was not ready—not for this conversation, not to hear his voice, not to risk losing the emotional control I had just started to regain.

I decided not to call him back—not yet. Not right now. I knew if I spoke to him too soon, I would unravel. And I refuse to let that happen.

Reflection & Analysis: Slight Signs of Emotional Freedom

Kellie's decision to reach out to her therapist demonstrates her determination to heal and take control of her emotional well-being: "It was time to heal, seek help, and regain my emotional strength." This step symbolizes a turning point, as she begins to prioritize her mental health. A critical realization occurs when Kellie acknowledges that she cannot control Rob's actions or thoughts: "Whether he had moved on, found someone new, or had emotionally checked out...those thoughts were tormenting me, and I had to let them go." This awareness is empowering, as it shifts her focus inward rather than dwelling on external factors.

Rob's unexpected call disrupts Kellie's sense of peace, illustrating how difficult it can be to maintain emotional boundaries in the face of lingering attachment: "My heart skipped a beat, and I froze. I was not sure whether to answer." Rob's voicemail, described as "calm and composed—so unaffected," emphasizes the emotional disparity between them. His detached demeanor contrasts sharply with the intense emotional turmoil Kellie has been experiencing, amplifying her sense of hurt and confusion. Kellie's choice not to return Rob's call reflects her growing strength and self-awareness: "I knew if I spoke to him too soon, I would unravel. And I refuse to let that happen." This decision underscores her commitment to protecting her emotional progress.

Kellie's proactive steps toward healing—seeking therapy and focusing on herself—are significant achievements, even if the process feels slow and uncertain. Each step represents progress, *no matter how small*. Rob's call is a stark reminder that emotional triggers can disrupt the healing process. However, Kellie's ability to pause and choose not to engage shows her growing resilience. Kellie's decision to prioritize her emotional well-being over immediate communication with Rob highlights the importance of setting boundaries during a vulnerable time. This choice allows her to maintain control and continue her healing journey.

Rob's detached tone reinforces Kellie's realization that his actions and emotions are out of her control. This disparity serves as a painful but necessary reminder of why the relationship ended. By choosing not to respond to Rob's voicemail, Kellie reclaims her power. This moment illustrates that she is no longer allowing Rob to dictate her emotional state or actions.

Journal Entry—Day 10: Mood—Guilt and Self-Reflection

This morning, I woke up with a familiar weight pressing on my chest—guilt. Not the reasonable kind, like forgetting someone's birthday or bailing on dinner plans. No, this was the ridiculous, soul-suffocating guilt of not calling Rob back. A man who, by the way, had no issue leaving me hanging for days.

I realized that I had been available on demand—texting back within seconds, shifting my plans to accommodate his ever-changing schedule, pretending it was totally fine that he got to call the shots. But somewhere along the way, the dynamic flipped. I went from being the one pursued to the one waiting. Waiting for him to text. Waiting for him to choose me. Waiting for whatever scraps of attention he was willing to throw my way.

Before Rob, I was different. I was confident, independent—a woman who loved her own damned company.

My days were filled with things that made me feel alive: driving down the Pacific Coast Highway with the windows down, stopping to shop in Newport Beach just because I could; sweating out stress in hot yoga, then rewarding myself with a Health Nut smoothie from Nekter Juice Bar; running wild with my Goldendoodle at the dog beach; and laughing over Sauvignon Blanc and prosciutto pizza with girlfriends at Snipe Island Crafthouse in Balboa. My life was a series of experiences that had nothing to do with waiting for a man to decide when I was worth his time.

Love, when it happened, was effortless. A fling here, a romance there—always fun, never suffocating. I wasn't the kind of woman who chased. And yet, somehow, I became her.

The One Who Got Away... but Never Left

Things started shifting long before Rob.

A few years earlier, there was Matt—a sniper marine with piercing blue eyes, a sculpted body, and an aura of intensity that could melt steel. The age gap (six years younger) didn't faze me. If anything, it made things more thrilling. He pursued me like I was the mission, said it was love at first sight. Told me my silky brunette hair and almond-shaped eyes had him hypnotized.

The beginning was nothing short of electric. Passion, adrenaline, and longing stretched between deployments that lasted months—sometimes years. With the distance came an undercurrent of tension. He had my heart, but I never fully had his presence.

And in his absence, life happened.

Enter: Scott

Scott was a surfer—carefree, golden-skinned, and effortless in a way Matt never was. We met on a dating app, and I told myself it was nothing serious. But weekends with him felt like stolen moments from a sun-drenched dream. Laguna Beach, sunset walks, saltwater kisses. It was simple. Easy. Real.

One night, as we toasted with mimosas under an orange-streaked sky, Scott looked at me and said it—the thing I wasn't ready to hear but somehow already knew.

"I think I'm falling for you."

And as if on cue, my phone buzzed.

Matt.

"Hey, Kellie! What are you up to right now?"

It was eerie, like he could feel the shift in the universe. Like he knew I was slipping away. He hadn't spoken to me in months, but suddenly, there he was—reappearing right when I was about to be free.

Matt never fully left, but he never fully stayed. And that's what kept me hooked.

The Pattern I Couldn't See:

Scott eventually moved across the country. Our story ended as quietly as it began. But Matt? He lingered, always sensing the moment I was about to let go. Just like Rob.

I see it now—the pattern.

I am drawn to men who give just enough to keep me tethered but never enough to keep me grounded. I hold on, even when they drift. I stay connected, even when they are absent. And somewhere in the process, I forget the version of me that never needed to wait.

But today, as I sit here, resisting the urge to dial Rob's number, I know one thing:

I'm done feeling guilty for reclaiming myself.

No more chasing. No more waiting. No more ghosts in my inbox.

I want the woman back—the one who lived for herself, not for the idea of being chosen. And this time, I won't let anyone—not Matt, not Rob, not the next emotionally unavailable guy who mistakes my heart for a revolving door—convince me to forget who the hell I am.

Reflection & Analysis: The Price of Availability: Reclaiming the Woman I Once Was

Kellie starts the entry with a feeling of guilt for not calling Rob back, which contrasts with her previous behavior of being available and accommodating. The guilt stems from her attachment to old patterns of being overly responsive in relationships, a pattern she now recognizes was not in her best interest:

"I realize that I had been available on demand—texting back within seconds, shifting my plans to accommodate his ever-changing schedule." This internal conflict highlights Kellie's awareness that her actions in relationships were often driven by a need to maintain connection, sometimes at the cost of her own emotional well-being.

Kellie contrasts her current feelings of guilt with her past sense of independence and confidence: "Before Rob, I was confident and independent." She reflects on the joy she derived from spending time alone, pursuing her passions, and engaging in meaningful activities. This shift in her relationship dynamics, from being confident and independent to feeling controlled and uncertain, represents a significant emotional loss. It emphasizes the emotional toll that Rob's behavior has taken on her.

Kellie reflects on her past relationships with Matt and Scott, noting that both men were emotionally unavailable in unusual ways. Both Matt and Rob showed interest, only to pull away or exert control, leaving Kelly confused and emotionally vulnerable. This realization that she attracts emotionally unavailable partners points to a deeper pattern in her romantic life that Kellie is beginning to recognize.

The repeated emotional unavailability she experiences has led to confusion, vulnerability, and the loss of her sense of self. Throughout the entry, Kellie expresses a desire to rediscover her former self—the confident woman who thrived on her own and enjoyed life on her own terms: "I miss the version of myself that thrived in independence and joy." This desire is not just a longing for the past but an active decision to reclaim her independence and emotional strength. It marks the beginning of a transformative journey, where she aims to take back control of her life and stop prioritizing relationships that drain her.

Kellie notes that in her relationship with Rob, the power dynamic shifted: "Our relationship shifted from him chasing me to him holding all the power." This realization indicates that Kellie is beginning to understand how Rob's behavior depleted her emotional energy. She was once confident and self-sufficient, but Rob's actions caused her to feel controlled and uncertain. This insight allows Kellie to recognize the manipulation in the relationship and begin disentangling herself from it.

By reflecting on her past relationships with Matt and Scott, Kellie recognizes a recurring pattern of attracting emotionally unavailable partners. This understanding is key to breaking the cycle of confusion and emotional vulnerability: "I attract emotionally unavailable partners and feel connected to them even when they are distant." Kellie is beginning to realize that her emotional attachment to unavailable partners stems from a deeper issue, which she will need to address if she wants to move forward in a healthier way.

The most profound insight in the entry is Kellie's desire to reclaim her independence and joy. She reflects on the activities and experiences she once enjoyed before relationships began to overshadow them. The journal entry reveals her growing recognition that she must prioritize her own well-being and happiness: "I want the woman back—the one who lived for herself, not for the idea of being chosen." This acknowledgment marks the beginning of a shift toward self-love and independence.

Kellie's decision not to call Rob back is a small but significant step toward reclaiming her emotional power. She is learning to set boundaries, prioritize her needs, and stop allowing her emotional state to be dictated by someone else's actions. By choosing not to re-engage Rob immediately, Kellie is honoring her emotional progress and re-inforcing her desire to move forward without being drawn back into the toxic dynamics of the past.

Kellie's recognition that she has been emotionally vulnerable and uncertain due to her attachment to emotionally unavailable partners signal her readiness for change. She is no longer willing to settle for relationships that don't nourish her and recognizes that this pattern is something she must break. Kellie's desire to rediscover her confident, independent self—shows her commitment to personal growth. This reflection points to her readiness to invest time and energy into herself, rather than waiting for validation or happiness from others.

This shift in mindset will empower Kellie to create a fulfilling life that is not dependent on the emotional availability or actions of others. The journal entry demonstrates Kellie's growing emotional intelligence. By reflecting on past relationships and recognizing her patterns, Kellie is beginning to understand the root of her emotional vulnerability. This self-awareness is a crucial step in her emotional healing journey, as it will help her make healthier choices moving forward.

Journal Entry—Day 11: Mood—Heavy, Conflicted, Resilient

This morning, I walked along Strands Beach, my feet sinking into damp sand as the tide crept in. The gray sky mirrored the heaviness in my chest, thick with a marine layer that pressed against my ribs like an unspoken grief. My friends walked beside me, their laughter soft, distant. They sensed my silence before they asked about Rob.

I exhaled, breaking the quiet. The heartbreak still sat heavy, an ache I couldn't name. They asked if he had reached out, and I nodded. He had. He called, and I let it ring. I let the voicemail sit there, untouched, like an uninvited ghost haunting my inbox. When I finally played it for them, Krisi tilted her head, listening intently.

"He sounds like he's holding back tears," she said.

Funny. Because in my ears, he sounded empty, detached, as if our love had been nothing but a passing inconvenience. It's strange, the way perception twists reality. How two people can hear the same words, yet pull entirely different meanings from them.

After the walk, I sat in my car, gripping my phone with white-knuckled hesitation. A sliver of defiance warred with the need for closure. My fingers shook as I dialed. He didn't answer.

A text came through minutes later. I'll call you at 5 p.m.

And so began the slow, torturous wait. The hours stretched long and cruel, my mind gnawing on every possibility, cycling through every imagined scenario. Would he apologize? Would he explain? Would he tell me he made a mistake?

When the phone finally rang, my breath caught in my throat. I answered with a soft, "Hey."

And just like that, we fell into small talk. Chit-chat. Meaningless words floating in the space between us. I told him about my walk. He told me about his day. We danced around the truth, skirting the edge of something raw and bleeding.

And then, the shift.

"I miss our time together," he admitted. "You were always so easy to talk to."

I swallowed. My pulse thrummed like war drums in my ears.

"So, what happened to us?" I asked. "What changed?"

A beat of silence. A slight tremor in his voice. And then the words that split my world apart:

"After you came back from Spain, I started losing physical attraction to you. You let yourself go. You got a little ... chubby."

A blade to the gut would have been kinder.

I froze, my mind recoiling, disbelief curdling into something darker—disgust, fury, devastation. The shallowness of it. The cruelty. The way he reduced me to flesh and bone, as if my worth had melted away with the softness of my body.

But I didn't break. Not then. Not yet.

I forced out something calm, something almost detached. "Okay. I see how you feel about me now."

The words felt foreign on my tongue, but they held my dignity intact.

Inside, I was unraveling.

The call ended. My composure fractured the moment I hung up. I collapsed, sobs tearing through me, my body shaking as I crumbled under the weight of his rejection.

But here's the thing.

As I lay there, shattered, something else stirred beneath the wreckage. A flicker of something... rebellious. Defiant. Free.

Because now I knew.

Rob never truly saw me. He never valued me—only the version of me that pleased his gaze. He didn't love the way I laughed too loud at my own jokes, or the way I cared for him even when he was at his weakest. He didn't cherish the woman who had once adored him despite his flaws—his aging body, his aches and pains, his imperfections.

But I did.

I had loved him as a whole person. He had loved me only in parts.

And that is not love.

That conversation, brutal as it was, set me free. I was done. Done with bending, with shrinking, with molding myself to fit inside a man's narrow, conditional affections.

I am reclaiming myself—bruised, but unbroken. My self-esteem may be in tatters, but my spirit is waking up, stretching its limbs, remembering its worth.

I refuse to be defined by someone else's fleeting attraction.

I deserve a love that sees me in every light, in every form, in every phase of my existence.

Reflection & Analysis: The Devastation of Shallow Love

This journal entry is more than a recollection of heartbreak—it is an autopsy of an illusion, a raw and unraveling of a relationship that was never built to last. It captures the moment where love, or at least the perception of it, crumbles under the weight of a single, shallow truth: Rob never truly valued Kellie as a whole person. His attraction was conditional, tethered only to the physical, and when that changed—however slightly—his desire disintegrated.

At its core, this entry is a narrative of disillusionment. Kellie begins in a state of emotional turmoil, carrying the weight of an unresolved breakup as she walks along Strands Beach with her friends. The setting itself plays an important symbolic role—the overcast sky, the thick marine layer, the taste of salt in the air—all external manifestations of the heaviness pressing against her chest. The environment reflects her inner state, mirroring the fog of confusion and grief she is wading through.

When Krisi listens to Rob's voicemail and hears a choked, emotional tone, it directly contrasts Kellie's own interpretation: indifference. This moment highlights an important theme—how perception shapes reality. It suggests that emotions, especially those clouded by pain, alter how we process events.

Did Rob truly sound remorseful? Or is it possible that Krisi, listening from a place of emotional distance, picked up on something Kellie was too hurt to acknowledge? Conversely, was Krisi romanticizing

Rob's tone, grasping for signs of depth that weren't really there? The ambiguity lingers, adding to the overall sense of emotional instability.

The afternoon spent waiting for Rob's call is an emotional battleground in itself. The time between the text message and 5 p.m. is stretched and torturous, mirroring the way unresolved love clings, refusing to loosen its grip. This wait is significant—it symbolizes how, even after a breakup, emotional ties keep a person tethered. She is caught in the limbo between longing and self-preservation, dreading the moment yet craving it, needing to know but fearing the truth.

When the call finally happens, the initial conversation is almost unnervingly casual. Small talk fills the space, a hesitant waltz around the inevitable. This is another powerful psychological moment—when two people who once shared intimacy suddenly find themselves behaving like strangers. The avoidance of deeper topics prolongs the pain, creating a tension that is both unbearable and yet strangely comfortable, as if delaying the truth will somehow keep the finality at bay.

The Devastation of Shallow Love—then, the moment of reckoning arrives.

"After you came back from Spain, I started losing physical attraction to you. You let yourself go. You got a little... chubby." This revelation is more than just cruel—it is a complete erasure of their emotional bond, reducing their entire relationship to something as fleeting as physical appearance. The weight of his words isn't just about body image; it is the gut-punch realization that what she thought was love was actually conditional desire. The depth she had assigned to their relationship was never real in his eyes.

Kellie's reaction is telling. Rather than an emotional outburst, she responds with a measured, dignified, almost detached, "Okay. I see how you feel about me now." This is an incredibly powerful moment of restraint—the kind of response that more weight than rage ever could. It is a silent surrender to the truth, a realization that there is no argument to be had because the battle was never fair to begin with. Rob's words don't just wound her; they expose the hollowness of their entire relationship.

After the call, her composure shatters. She allows herself to feel the depth of rejection, collapsing under its weight, sobbing, shaking, unraveling. This moment is the necessary breakdown before the breakthrough. It is the body processing the emotional violence of being discarded so superficially. But what follows is something extraordinary: a quiet rebellion. Amidst the grief, a flicker of something else arises—anger, yes, but also a deep and growing realization. This is her way out. This is freedom disguised as pain.

She reflects on how she loved Rob through his imperfections—the way she cared for him even when he wasn't at his best. She recalls his complaints about his aching body, his aging, his own physical decline. And yet, her love did not waver. Herein lies the ultimate contrast: she loved him beyond the surface, but he could not do the same for her. And with that understanding, she begins to reclaim her worth.

This journal entry doesn't just document heartbreak—it documents rebirth. It begins in confusion, spirals into devastation, and ends in the first steps of liberation. The final realization is the most powerful: Rob was never the one. He was simply the lesson. His rejection, while deeply painful, was also the clearest proof that she deserves more. That she is not a body to be assessed, but a soul to be cherished. That the right love will see her in all forms, in all seasons, through all phases of life.

The closing emotion is one of conflicted empowerment. There is still grief, still insecurity, but it is tinged with a quiet defiance. She is stepping away from the wreckage, battle-scarred but unbowed. And perhaps, for the first time since the breakup, Kellie chooses herself.

Journal Entry—Day 12: Mood—Reflective and poignant, tinged with vulnerability and a sense of self-discovery.

When Rob said, "After you came back from Spain, I started to lose physical attraction to you. I felt like you let yourself go," his words struck with the precision of a blade, clean and final. There was no way to misinterpret them, no soft edges to cushion the blow. He didn't hesitate, didn't flinch. Meanwhile, I sat there, stunned, breathless—reduced to nothing but flesh, weight, appearance.

I had just returned from a trip that had once lived only in my dreams, a journey across the world to a place I had longed to experience, a pilgrimage back to my Catholic roots. Spain was supposed to be mine. It was supposed to be a reclamation of self, a moment where I stood on foreign soil, fully alive, fully free. And yet, I had let him creep into the cracks of my experience, filling spaces that should have been mine alone.

I thought our connection deepened with every message I sent, every photo I shared. In my mind, I wasn't traveling alone—Rob was right there with me. At least, I had convinced myself of that. I chronicled my days as if they were love letters to him: My departure from LAX, the weight of excitement and anticipation in my chest; My layover in Madrid, texting him from an unfamiliar airport café, feeling a rush of comfort when his name lit up my screen; My first taste of tinto de verano at a bustling tapas bar, the coolness of the drink mingling with the warmth of the Spanish sun; The streets of Seville—illuminated by the golden glow of the Aurora light show, lined with vendors selling freshly sliced jamón and fragrant paellas. I wanted him to see it all.

But did he even care? Or was he merely humoring me, scanning through my photos absentmindedly, already disengaging while I held on tighter? Had I been talking to a man who had already made up his mind?

I had told myself that I was traveling for me, that this was my solo adventure, my personal journey. But if that were true, then why did I constantly reach for my phone, checking for his response? Why did my heart skip when he replied, sink when he didn't? I was there, in Spain, yet a part of me was still tethered to him, waiting for my experiences to be validated through his eyes.

That's the part that stings the most—not just his words, but the realization that I had unknowingly placed my joy in his hands, waiting for him to confirm that my life was worth experiencing.

So when he said it—when he uttered those shallow, thoughtless words—I felt like you let yourself go—the pain wasn't just in the insult. It was in the confirmation of a terrible truth.

He never saw me. Not really. Not the woman who had traveled across the world alone.

Not the woman who had wandered through the historic Semana Santa processions, watching the artful floats pass by, absorbing the haunting echoes of the Saetas sung from balconies. Not the woman who had stepped into that trip with a heart wide open, longing for connection, for meaning, for something greater than herself. All he saw was a little weight gain.

His words cut deep, not just because they were cruel, but because they forced me to confront the parts of myself I had ignored for too long. I had been clinging—to him, to his approval, to the illusion that his validation made my experiences more meaningful. I had turned my independence into a performance, living my life while simultaneously documenting it for his attention.

And for what?

So he could casually discard me when the shape of my body no longer suited him?

Is this what attachment does when it turns toxic? It makes you believe that you are only as valuable as someone else's ability to desire you. That love is something you must earn, maintain, protect—even at the cost of yourself.

I see it now, so clearly, as if the fog has finally lifted.

I had built him into something greater than he was. I had assigned meaning to every text, every interaction, convincing myself that our connection was deeper than it ever actually was.

But now?

Now, I rewrite the story. Rob didn't lose attraction because I let myself go.

Rob lost attraction because he was never capable of loving me in the first place. A man who measures love in inches and pounds was never someone who deserved my soul.

The Real Loss—It wasn't my body that changed—it was my perception of him.

And that's the real tragedy here. Not the extra weight, not the hurtful words, but the fact that I had spent so much time believing he was something more.

I look back now, at my time in Spain, and I reclaim those moments. I was there. I existed in those places, in that air, under that sky. And Rob? He was never really there at all.

Reflection & Analysis: Shattered Illusions—A Wake-Up Call to Reclaim My Self-Worth

Rob's words, "I started to lose physical attraction to you. You let yourself go," are not just hurtful—they are dehumanizing. With one sentence, he reduces an entire relationship, an entire person, to something temporary, conditional, disposable. It is a confirmation of every silent insecurity that lingered in the back of her mind, now spoken out loud with casual cruelty.

The Brutality of a Shallow Love: His statement doesn't acknowledge the shared moments, the emotional investment, or the deep care she poured into him. Instead, it strips everything down to aesthetics—as if the love between them only existed within the confines of her physical form.

This isn't just about losing Rob—it's about losing the illusion that what they had was built on anything real. That's the true heartbreak.

One of the most powerful realizations in this entry is how deeply intertwined her self-worth was with Rob's perception of her. The Spain trip, which should have been a bold, independent adventure, was in many ways a performance—something she lived through his eyes, even though he was miles away.

The Illusion of Connection: Kellie sent photos, narrated her experiences, reached for his presence in a place where she should have been fully present for herself. But was Rob ever truly on the other side, feeling closer to her? Or was she just projecting, filling his absence with hopeful meaning?

The Moment She Realizes It: Looking back, she sees it clearly now. She wasn't just living the experience—she was curating it for him. And in doing so, she robbed herself of the pure joy of simply being. The weight of this realization is heavier than the heartbreak itself—because it isn't just about Rob anymore. It's about how she has lost herself in the pursuit of being wanted.

What makes this journal entry so powerful is that Kellie does not stay in self-pity. There is a shift—a spark of something fierce, rebellious, defiant. At first, she is wounded. Then, she is disgusted. Disgusted with his shallowness. Disgusted with herself for giving him so much power. And in that disgust, the tide begins to turn.

The Illusion Shatters: She reflects on how she had always seen Rob as someone who valued her—but he never did. She loved him beyond the surface, but he was incapable of doing the same. And that is the final breaking point.

This is where the healing begins. Not in letting go of Rob—but in letting go of the belief that his opinion ever had any bearing on her worth. By the end of this entry, Rob is small. He is no longer the man whose attention dictates her happiness. He is a wake-up call, not a loss.

She sees him now—not as a love lost, but as a lesson learned.

She is reclaiming Spain—not as a shared experience, but as hers.

She is choosing herself—not in rebellion, but in liberation.

Her words carry a quiet but potent power—the power of detachment. This isn't a grand, cinematic "I'm over him" moment, but something more real, more subtle:

A realization that the only thing she truly lost... was the illusion. And in that loss, she finds herself again.

Journal Entry—Day 13: Mood—Emotional exhaustion, mixed with a hint of emerging clarity and resolve.

I t has been two weeks since Rob and I broke up, and today I felt the first touch of clarity, albeit a painful one. For the first time, it truly hit me: Rob is not coming back. All this time, I have been analyzing every detail, rehashing every moment, replaying all the things I might have missed, as though dissecting it would change the reality that he's already gone.

I spent so much energy sulking, agonizing over his motives, but it does not matter now. What difference does it make to obsess over someone who so easily walked away from what I thought we shared?

I had imagined a future with him—our relationship felt like it had depth, promise, and genuine connection. I now see, though painfully, that his intentions may have been entirely different. I cannot shake the feeling that he used me emotionally, pulled me in with calculated charm and seductive promises. It was power play, and I fell hard, allowing myself to become wrapped around his finger until I lost sight of my own power.

He left me feeling weak and trapped, entangled in emotions I cannot seem to unravel. Why am I not furious about what he did to me? He manipulated my trust, yet here I am, struggling to untangle my emotions from the memories of him. There is a strange, twisted void that nothing else seems able to fill right now.

No other experience, no other relationship or routine feels like it can compare to what Rob's presence brought to my life. I keep replaying the sense of safety I felt with him in my mind, even if that safety was an illusion. Somehow, I am finding it so hard to get over him, and that dependency feels suffocating, like a weight I cannot shake. It is painful to admit, but I was so used to having him as the anchor in my life, someone to lean on, someone to share my experiences with, someone to simply be there.

And today, I faced my worst fear: it really is over. There are so many emotions I cannot even begin to process. Part of me feels lost in silence, like I cannot summon the words to say what has been left unsaid or ask the questions I never dared to ask. There are countless unanswered questions, but the one thing I am clear on is that I never want to be in this position again. The pain of losing someone you trusted with your heart is too much, and the toll it has taken on me is profound. I do not want to feel this helpless again.

Right now, I feel like I have lost a crucial part of myself. Rob became a crutch, someone I relied on not only for companionship but to help make sense of things and give life a certain vibrancy. Now, without him, I feel like I'm missing a piece of myself that I don't know how to replace. How do I rebuild interest, excitement, and passion for life without him by my side?

The truth is, I do not know. But I know this much—I do not want to feel this disempowered again. Somewhere in the silence and the hurt, I must find a way to re-discover myself, to reclaim my strength and sense of self-worth, independent of anyone else's validation. I can rebuild from here, day by day, with a promise to myself that I will never let someone take away this much of my power again. For now, I must sit with the pain, let it remind me that I am strong enough to heal, and remind myself that this is not the end but rather the beginning of finding my way back to me.

Reflection & Analysis: The Price of Attachment—Finding Strength After Loss

Kellie is deeply hurt, grappling with loss and confusion after placing so much of her self worth and happiness in her relationship with Rob. Her journey highlights the depth of attachment she developed, making Rob almost essential to her daily life and sense of purpose. By reliving memories and moments from the relationship, she begins to realize the cost of having intertwined her identity so tightly with someone else.

The initial feeling of loss and confusion is a common part of many breakups, particularly when someone invests heavily in the relationship emotionally. Kellie struggles with the dependency she built, admitting that life feels dull without Rob, yet she recognizes the impact this reliance has had on her. The disillusionment she feels in realizing

Rob may not have seen or valued her for who she truly is propels her toward reflection, setting the foundation for healing.

This is the first step in Kellie's journal entry toward reclaiming her sense of self. By acknowledging her feelings of powerlessness and her desire to *avoid this pain again*, she is moving toward an understanding of what she needs to heal—personal strength, self-validation, and independence. The experience is painful, yet within it, there's a glimmer of hope and resilience.

This moment of clarity serves as a reminder that healing, while uncomfortable, is a journey of rediscovering one's own value and building inner strength. Kellie's realization that this may be a beginning rather than an ending shows a burgeoning readiness to explore life on her own terms, reinforcing the power of self-discovery and growth after loss.

Kellie is grappling with feelings of abandonment and disillusionment, mourning both the loss of her relationship and the personal power she feels she sacrificed. There is a palpable sense of grief, intensified by her realization of dependency on Rob and the void his absence has created in her daily life. Yet, amid the sadness and frustration, there is a faint shift toward self-awareness and determination. Kellie' s reflections reveal an underlying desire to understand her emotional state and prevent similar situations in the future, suggesting the start of an empowering, albeit difficult, journey toward healing. The complex mix of heartbreak and self-realization shapes a somber yet reflective mood and an air of Kellie's resilience.

Journal Entry—Day 14: Mood—Tentative Resilience, Mixed with Determination and Pain

S itting with the pain, I felt a pull to act—something to ease the weight of this heartbreak, if only a little. I'm still grieving the loss of Rob and the relationship, but today, I resolved to start finding my way out of this. Somewhere within the silence and sadness, I know I must begin rediscovering who I am, reclaiming my strength and my worth, independent of anyone's validation. I'm not rushing; I'll rebuild slowly, but with a promise to myself that no one will ever take this much of my power again. For now, I'll let the pain settle as a reminder that I'm resilient enough to heal. This isn't the end but the beginning of finding my way back to myself.

In between moments of journaling, I sketched out a "get over him" challenge—a list of small, tangible steps I could take. The first was to delete photos of Rob, of us, from my phone. Each swipe hurt, deleting memories of happy moments together, but I couldn't keep those reminders everywhere I looked. For now, they're backed up just in case I want to look someday, but I don't need that today.

I left him unblocked in my contacts and felt the strange relief of knowing there's no social media connection between us. Sometimes I regret not having him there just to post a few "revenge" pictures or quotes—but I know deep down that wouldn't really help. Disappearing for a while, giving myself the space to heal without him in view, feels more genuine.

To help fill this void, I'm throwing myself into new routines. I signed up for daily yoga and gym classes, aiming to turn my emotional pain into physical resilience. Today, I pushed through a couple of back-to-back yoga sculpt classes, leaving the studio sore and exhausted, with barely any energy left to overanalyze or mourn. By the time I got home, my body was so worn that I fell straight into bed and, for the first time in a while, slept soundly. This process is anything but easy, but this is how I'll slowly find strength and peace in my own company once again.

Reflection & Analysis: Reclaiming My Light

Kellie feels a deep sadness and lingering heartbreak from the breakup but also expresses a budding resolve to move forward. There is a sense of quiet strength as she takes steps toward healing, even as she feels the sting of painful memories. This combination of sorrow, hope, and cautious optimism creates an emotional tone that feels both heavy with loss and lightened by small acts of self-care and empowerment.

The struggle is evident—though deeply hurt, Kellie is beginning to take the reins of her own recovery. The act of deleting photos, for instance, while painful, represents a crucial step in letting go of the past, even though part of Rob is still tied to memories she isn't ready to fully release. This ambivalence—saving photos on a backup just in case—is a tender reminder that healing is rarely straightforward.

What also stands out is Kellie's choice not to block Rob or indulge in revenge fantasies. This restraint is significant, showing an instinct toward genuine healing rather than getting caught in reactive or out-ward-focused behaviors. It signals maturity, suggesting she wants to free herself from pain rather than deepen it with unresolved bitterness or resentment. The decision to dive into yoga and physical activity is another symbol of positive transformation, translating emotional hurt into physical movement, which may give Kellie both a new focus and a release from mental anguish.

Underlying all these choices is Kellie's understanding that true healing will take time and patience. She is beginning to grasp that the void left by this relationship isn't something that needs to be filled with another person but rather by reconnecting with *her own sense of purpose, self-worth, and joy*. Kellie expresses a budding desire not just to move on but to emerge from this experience stronger and more self-assured.

Kellie's journal entry is about reclaiming self-respect, cultivating resilience, and accepting that the journey forward will involve sitting with pain as well as taking steps to rise above it. This reflection, though raw, hints at growth and an eventual renewal of Kellie's sense of iden-tity and strength.

Journal Entry Day 15: mood – mix of longing, pain, and a sense of resignation

It's unsettling—Rob insulted me, discarded me, reduced me to nothing more than flesh and vanity—and yet, I am still here, trapped in the ruins of what we were. It's been two weeks, but today the pain feels sharper, almost unbearable, like an open wound that refuses to close.

Why do I still crave him? I tell myself I should be angry, that I should hate him for his shallow words, but anger doesn't erase longing. I miss the way he made me laugh, the playful banter, the stupid memes, the way his voice softened late at night when sleep blurred the edges of our conversations. I miss the way he made cocktails, the way he sent me photos from his bike rides, the way his presence felt like an anchor—until it didn't. Last night, as I was driving home, "Everywhere" by Fleetwood Mac came on the radio, and it nearly wrecked me.

That song. Our song. The one we danced to on a warm summer night, swaying under a blanket of stars, caught in the moment as Fleetwood Mac played live in the background. I remember the way his arms wrapped around me, the way he whispered against my hair, "God, you are beautiful."

I close my eyes, and I can still feel the weight of that moment—the music, the laughter, the heat of the summer air against our skin. And then, just as quickly, it's gone, replaced by the sickening realization that none of it meant as much to him as it did to me.

It wasn't just a song. It was a promise. A feeling. A night where time slowed, and I thought, this is real. And yet, here I am, discarded, forgotten. The words he once said—"I get excited thinking of the day with you. I see you everywhere, in everything."—now feel like cruel jokes, echoes of a love that never held weight beyond the moment.

That summer, he fixed my motorcycle helmet on my head, adjusting the strap carefully, gazing at me like I was the most breathtaking thing he had ever seen. The way he looked at me that night—I believed it. Now, I wonder if it was ever real at all.

Now, my life is littered with reminders of him, like landmines I can't avoid. Every song, every scent, every quiet moment seems to whisper his name. And the worst part? Despite everything, despite how he made me feel small, I still want him to want me.

That's the part that disgusts me the most.

I gave up so much of myself for him. Let him dictate my happiness, control my emotions, ration out his affection like it was something I had to earn. I lived for the thrill of his attention, shackled to the high of being wanted, terrified of what it meant when he pulled away. I see it now—the version of myself that shrank in his presence, the one who was always waiting, always chasing. I want to reach out so badly. Just to hear his voice, just to pull him back into my world for one fleeting moment. But I won't. I can't. Because I know what will happen. I'll hear him speak in that same indifferent tone, I'll feel the void between us stretch wider, and I'll regret it before the call even ends.

Reaching out won't fix anything. It will only prove how little I've let go.

So today, I made a promise to myself.

I will take back my power.

I will be the main character in my life, not some side plot in his.

I will not depend on a man's validation to feel whole.

I will not shrink for anyone ever again.

I wrote those words in my journal, read them back to myself, again and again, willing them to feel real. But truthfully, I don't believe them yet. Not entirely.

But maybe if I keep saying them, keep writing them, keep forcing myself to stand in the wreckage without calling for him, they'll sink in. Maybe one day, I'll say them and actually mean them.

Krisi called today, her voice a break in the chaos, reminding me to RSVP to Debi's wedding in Texas next month. A reminder that life is still moving forward, even when I feel stuck.

Maybe it's a small distraction, but right now, distraction feels like survival. Maybe the thought of choosing a dress, booking a flight, pretending to be okay in a room full of people who don't know I'm breaking, will be enough to push me one step forward.

My healing is slow. Some days, I feel almost normal—like I've climbed out of the wreckage, like I can finally breathe without him. And then there are days like today, when grief slams into me, relentless and unforgiving, pulling me back under.

But even on the worst days, I am still here.

And if I can just keep choosing myself, even in the smallest of ways, maybe one day, I won't have to try so hard. Maybe one day, I will wake up and realize that I am whole—without him, without his words, without his gaze.

Maybe one day, I will be free.

Reflection & Analysis: Echoes of 'Everywhere': Navigating Heartache and Healing

Kellie feels the acute ache of missing Rob, expressed through vivid memories and emotional cravings for connection. There is also a strong undertone of a frustrating sense of betrayal and self-awareness as she grapples with how much control she gave away in the relationship.

One of the most powerful aspects of this entry is the contrast between past and present—the way memories still live and breathe in Kellie's mind, while Rob has already discarded them. "Everywhere" by Fleetwood Mac is more than just a song. It is a moment, a feeling, a night when love felt infinite—when she and Rob danced beneath the stars, lost in the music, lost in each other. His words from that night—"I see you everywhere, in everything"—were once a promise. Now, they ring hollow, exposed for what they were: temporary sentiment, not lasting devotion.

The motorcycle helmet scene is an intimate snapshot, a fleeting moment when she believed she was adored, cherished, seen. But what does it mean if a man can look at you like that one day and leave you behind the next? The depth of her love is evident—the problem is, it was one-sided. What she felt, what she remembers, was real to her. But for Rob, it was fleeting, conditional, easily replaced. And that's where the real pain lies—not just in losing him, but in realizing he never held the same weight for her as she did for him.

One of the most relatable aspects of this entry is the way grief and logic clash—how Kellie knows she should let go but still craves him anyway. She wants to reach out, but she knows better. She knows that if she does, she will hear that same indifferent tone in his voice, confirming the painful truth: he has already moved on.

She knows his words should disgust her, yet she still aches for his attention. This is not stupidity—it's human nature. We long for closure, for meaning, for the reassurance that what we felt wasn't just in our heads. This back-and-forth is one of the most painfully real parts of moving on—the logical mind knows the truth, but the heart refuses to accept it. Some days, she feels okay. Other days, a song, a smell, a fleeting memory rips her wide open again. Healing is not linear. And Kellie is in the in-between—the space where she is still tied to the past but reaching for the future.

And maybe that wedding invitation is a gift in disguise—a chance to escape the familiar spaces that trigger memories of Rob, connect with new people, and refocus Kellie's energy on new beginnings. This journey is challenging, but it builds a foundation of self-respect and self-care that Kellie will need as she undergoes a breakup to build her resilience and capabilities of finding happiness based on her own terms.

Journal Entry—Day 16: Mood—conflicted, vulnerable, and anguished, with a subtle undercurrent of growing awareness.

There had always been subtle signs of Rob's lack of genuine intentions toward me. He kept me at a distance, carefully controlling the relationship within the boundaries he set—always dangling the prize of something without ever truly offering certainty or reassurance. It felt like a game, with him maintaining just enough connection to keep me hooked.

Most of our interactions were through text updates or glimpses into his life, his exciting adventures, the family, and friends he visited, the breathtaking scenes he captured on his bike rides and skiing trips.

I was enamored, entertained, and deeply impressed by the world he seemed to inhabit.

I admired Rob's adventurous spirit and the beauty of his life, and I clung to those updates, convincing myself that his willingness to share them meant I was a part of it all. I grew dependent on those small glimpses, wondering where he would go next and when, if ever, I would truly be included in his adventures.

At first, I told myself to be patient. I rationalized that it was too soon to worry about where I stood in his life. I was overthinking things. Rob was showing me a world I could one day be part of. I told myself to wait, to let the relationship progress naturally.

But as months passed, I found myself stuck in a cycle of wondering and questioning. Where was this all leading? Rob's assurances were vague, his commitments uncertain. He kept me dangling with promises of seeing each other "soon"—a week here, two weeks there. When he returned from his trips, I'd feel ecstatic about the time we spent together. The highs were intoxicating. But after those moments, the pattern repeated: the waiting, the uncertainty, and the inevitable crash when days passed with no clarity about our next meeting or the future of our relationship.

Rob maintained contact through daily texts, but they offered no true security or sense of where we stood. There were no conversations about what we were building together. It was just updates—what he was doing, what I was doing. When my doubts crept in, I silenced them, convincing myself to relax, to ease into things, to give it time. I wanted so desperately to believe that this was just the natural progression of a relationship.

What I didn't realize was how much this uncertainty was quietly dismantling me. The hope I clung to became entangled with heartache. The guessing game consumed me, slowly eroding my sense of self-worth. I started to question myself: Am I worthy of Rob's love? Am I the kind of woman who can capture his heart?

I did not notice how much I had changed. I had gone from being an independent, strong woman to someone fixated on winning Rob's affection. My world started to revolve around him—what he liked, what he wanted, what would make him happy. My own happiness became dependent on his attention, his validation. Every time he reached out, it felt like a lifeline. And when he didn't, I felt like I was drowning.

The obsession began to gnaw at my spirit, fueled by the highs of his attention and the crushing lows of his distance. The pursuit of his commitment consumed me, but deep down, I knew the truth: this love was not restoring me. It was not reviving me. Instead, it left me feeling insecure, unsettled, and increasingly unworthy.

Reflection & Analysis: Bound by Uncertainty - The Highs, Lows, and Lessons of Losing Myself

Kellie reflects on her internal conflict and emotional vulnerability as she grapples with the highs and lows of a relationship marked by inconsistency, uncertainty, and dependency. It portrays a deep personal struggle with themes of self-worth, emotional attachment, and the corrosive effects of an unbalanced dynamic.

Kellie oscillates between hope and doubt, rationalizing her feelings while grappling with the inconsistency of Rob's behavior. There is a yearning for clarity and validation while simultaneously feeling the weight of uncertainty. Kellie reveals her emotional dependency on Rob, highlighting feelings of insecurity and a loss of self-worth. Her world seems to revolve around Rob's actions and affections, leaving her exposed to the highs and lows of his unpredictable behavior.

There is a sense of deep heartache and frustration over the lack of peace and stability in the relationship. Kellie's reflection on her insecurity and loss of independence adds a layer of sorrow and disillusionment. Despite the pain, there's a glimmer of realization in Kellie's tone. She is beginning to recognize the detrimental impact of this relationship on her confidence and identity, though she hasn't yet reached full acceptance or resolution.

Overall, the mood is emotionally raw, dominated by inner turmoil and the struggle to reconcile the allure of love with the painful realities of a toxic relationship. Kellie's journey speaks to the painful realization that her emotional well-being has become tied to Rob's actions, leaving her feeling powerless and consumed by insecurity.

This dependency has led Kellie to question her self-worth, showing how a *lack of clarity* and commitment in a relationship can *erode* one's confidence and sense of identity. The oscillation between hope and despair highlights the addictive nature of Kellie's connection to Rob, where brief moments of happiness are overshadowed by prolonged periods of uncertainty and emotional distress.

Kellie's vulnerability is apparent as she recounts how her focus shifted from her own needs and desires to an overwhelming preoccupation with pleasing Rob and gaining his affection. This shift is both relatable and heartbreaking, illustrating the danger of losing oneself in the pursuit of validation from another person. Kellie's growing awareness, though still clouded by pain, suggests the early stages of self-reflection and the potential for eventual healing.

The passage captures the damaging effects of an imbalanced power dynamic in a relationship. Rob's lack of reassurance and his tendency to keep Kellie "on the hook" has created a cycle of highs and lows that fuels Kellie's emotional dependency. The use of phrases like "slowly destroying me" and "shattering my confidence" emphasizes the profound toll this dynamic has taken on Kellie's mental and emotional state.

Kellie's shift from independence to obsession underscores how unresolved uncertainty can dismantle a person's sense of agency. She moves from being a confident, self-assured individual to someone who questions her worth and molds her own happiness around the unpredictable attention of another. This transformation is a powerful commentary on how relationships, when unhealthy, can distort one's priorities and self-perception.

However, there is a glimmer of self-awareness in Kellie's reflection. She begins to recognize that the relationship is not "restoring and reviving" her but instead causing emotional harm. This awareness, though painful, is a crucial step toward reclaiming her self-worth and healing. Kellie's experience serves as a poignant reminder of the importance of self-worth and emotional boundaries in relationships. True love should be a source of stability, growth, and mutual respect—not a *rollercoaster* of uncertainty and self-doubt.

Kellie's acknowledgment of her insecurity and dependency lays the foundation for a journey toward rediscovering her independence and building a life untethered from another's validation. While the pain is palpable, the passage hints at resilience and the possibility of renewal through self-reflection and self-compassion.

Journal Entry—Day 17: Mood—introspective, melancholic, and conflicted, with an undercurrent of self-awareness and painful realization.

I don't know when it started—the unraveling, the slow erosion of my confidence, the feeling of losing myself while chasing something that was never real. I only know that one day, I was the woman he pursued, the woman he desired, the woman he made feel wanted... and then, just as quickly, I was the woman left waiting.

Waiting for his texts.

Waiting for our next plans.

Waiting for him to choose me.

The weeks turned into months, and doubt seeped in like a slow poison. His words dangled just enough hope to keep me tethered, but his actions told the truth—I was not a priority, just an option. After his trips, I would wait—always waiting—for him to reach out, for him to set the next time, for him to decide when I was worthy of his attention again.

And when he finally did?

The highs were blinding. Intoxicating. Like he had pressed reset on my insecurities, erasing every moment I had spent doubting him, doubting us. In those moments, I felt chosen. And that feeling? It was a drug.

But the crash always followed. And I was the one left picking up the pieces.

October: The Fantasy Before the Fall

October was a dream and a deception all at once. I remember the thrill of Halloween, the way I dressed up as Daphne from Scooby-Doo, my red hair vibrant under the neon lights, my purple heels clicking against pavement as we laughed through the night.

Rob loved the way I looked—he said so over and over, his eyes hungry, his hands pulling me close. That night, I felt it, the rush of being seen, being wanted. I thought I had him. I thought we had something real.

But after the high came the silence. His pullback was always so subtle, so calculated. Not enough to let me go completely—just enough to keep me reaching. I could feel it, the shift in energy, the widening gap between us. But still, I questioned myself instead of him.

Is he just busy? Am I expecting too much? Is this normal? Is he playing games? Is there someone else? I already knew the answer. I just wasn't ready to accept it.

November: The Text That Broke Me

And then came November.

"We are not the match I'm looking for, and I'd like to entertain dating." It was so clinical. So detached. A message that shattered me without even trying. There it was—my worst fear, typed out like a business transaction.

But even as my stomach dropped, I forced myself to hold onto my dignity. "I never thought we were a perfect match either. You are free to go." And suddenly, just like that, I was free.

But then—why did it still hurt so goddamn much?

Rob replied instantly, as if my composure had caught him off guard. "I never meant to hurt you." And that's when I knew. He didn't want to be with me. But he didn't want to let me go either. I should have left it there. I should have blocked his number, burned the bridge, let the ashes scatter into nothing. But heartbreak doesn't make you logical. It makes you desperate.

The Push, The Pull, The Addiction

I thought breaking things off would give me closure. But instead, it gave me an emptiness that I didn't know how to fill. And just when I started to stitch myself back together, Rob reached out again. And I let him back in. Like a fool. Like a woman who should have known better. What kind of woman takes back a man who already left her once? A woman who still believed she could change the ending.

And so, the cycle continued.

The push. The pull. The fire and the freeze.

The fleeting moments where he made me feel like the only woman in the world.

The cold spaces in between, where I felt like a stranger in his life. And I adapted. I trained myself to live for the highs, to survive the lows. I learned to shrink, to mold, to fit the shape of the woman I thought he wanted.

Every time he pulled away, I wanted him more. Every time he came back, I thought—this time, he'll stay. But this was not love. It was not restorative. Not fulfilling.

It was an addiction. An addiction to being wanted. An addiction to proving my worth. An addiction to chasing someone who would never truly be mine. And it cost me everything. Losing Myself to a Love That Wasn't Real I stopped seeing myself clearly.

Somewhere along the way, I lost the woman I used to be. The woman who had boundaries. The woman who didn't wait around for breadcrumbs. The woman who knew her worth. I wasn't her anymore. I had become someone else entirely—someone consumed by a love that was never really love at all.

I lost myself in the illusion of us.

And the worst part? I let it happen.

Reflection & Analysis: Chasing Illusions—The Cost of Love & Self Loss

Kellie's journal entry is a deeply personal and unfiltered descent into the psychological grip of an on-again, off-again relationship—one where hope, desire, and addiction keep her tethered to something that was never real. It is a brutally honest account of love as a cycle of highs and withdrawals, a relationship that mimicked the rush of a drug—intoxicating in its best moments, soul-destroying in its worst.

What makes this entry so emotionally immersive and painfully real is that Kellie knows what is happening to her, but she still can't break free. She sees the pattern, the manipulation, the way she's losing herself—but knowing something is toxic doesn't always mean you're ready to let it go.

Kellie's relationship with Rob wasn't built on stability—it was built on anticipation, on the thrill of being chosen and the devastation of being discarded. "After his trips, I would wait for him to reach out..." This is where the power imbalance started. Rob dictated the rhythm of their relationship—when they saw each other, when he acknowledged her, when he gave her attention. "The highs were incredibly intense, joyful, intoxicating!" This is why she stayed.

The emotional reward was so intense that it made the lows feel survivable. The love she was getting wasn't consistent, but when it was there, it was powerful enough to make her forget the pain. This is the hallmark of emotional manipulation—pull away just enough to create longing, then return just before the other person detaches. Rob didn't have to force her to stay—he just had to keep her hoping.

October: The Fantasy vs. Reality—Halloween serves as a symbol of the duality in their relationship—a night where she was adored, where she felt desired, followed by the inevitable pullback. "That night, I was over the moon, feeling like I'd found something real with Rob." The use of "real" is important. She wanted to believe in him, believe that he meant what he showed in those moments. "But soon after, the highs faded, replaced by his silence." The silence is the real Rob. The absence, the uncertainty—that was always who he was. But she held onto the fantasy instead.

The contrast between the intimacy of that night and the cold reality that followed highlights the emotional chaos of loving someone who thrives on distance. She wasn't in love with who Rob was—she was in love with the version of him she experienced in fleeting moments.

November—The Text That Confirmed Everything. When Rob sent the text: "We are not the match I'm looking for, and I'd like to entertain dating." He finally said what his actions had been screaming all along. It was blunt, transactional, devoid of emotion. It confirmed Kellie's worst fear—she was never enough for him. And yet, even in rejection, he still wanted to keep his options open.

What makes this moment so painfully relatable is that instead of begging or falling apart, Kellie responded with dignity. "I never thought we were a perfect match either. You are free to go." This is the moment where she should have reclaimed herself. This was her exit. But closure doesn't come from words—it comes from the absence of longing. And Kellie wasn't ready to let go yet.

When Rob immediately followed up with: "I never meant to hurt you." He reminded her that he still had control. And that's all it took. Because he wasn't just rejecting her—he was leaving a door open. And that door was all she needed to keep hoping. The Cycle of Emotional Addiction: "I thought breaking things off would give me closure. But instead, it gave me an emptiness I didn't know how to fill."

This is one of the most brutally honest lines in the entry. Letting go didn't set her free—it created a void. And when something has consumed your identity, the void feels worse than the pain of staying. "And just when I started to stitch myself back together, Rob reached out again." This is the moment of relapse. Because he always knew when to return—when she was close to healing, close to walking away. "What kind of woman takes back a man who already left her once?"

The shame, the self-loathing, the inner conflict between logic and longing. She knows better, but knowing is not enough. The push, the pull. The addiction to the highs.

"The fleeting moments where he made me feel like the only woman in the world."

"The cold spaces in between, where I felt like a stranger in his life."

This isn't love. This isn't even about Rob anymore. This is about Kellie's battle with herself.

The Ultimate Cost is losing herself—"I shaped my life around his whims and desires." This is the darkest part of the entry. She didn't just love him. She became dependent on him to define her worth. "This was not love. It was not restorative or fulfilling." A moment of clarity. She can finally name it: this was never love. It was need. It was survival. "I lost myself in the illusion of us." The final, painful truth. She wasn't just chasing Rob. She was chasing a version of herself she believed could finally be worthy of his love. And that's the tragedy.

She lost herself trying to prove to him that she was worth choosing. Kellie's entry is messy, painful, deeply human. It captures the slow burn of emotional dependence, the intoxicating nature of intermittent reinforcement, and the gut-wrenching realization that she has been fighting for something that was never meant for her. This is the breaking point. Not in the way she'd expected—not a dramatic goodbye, not an empowering speech. But in the quiet realization that she is exhausted. That she is done being at war with herself. And that's where real healing begins.

Journal Entry Day 18: Mood~ Hopeful Yet, Cautiously optimistic, With Undercurrents of Tension And Unease

As I reminisced about those times when we got back together, I gave in to Rob's apologies and decided to give us another chance. This time, things felt different—Rob was more consistent, and our interactions, dates, and meetups became more frequent. It felt like I had finally won him over, and for the first time, it seemed as though our relationship was heading towards something serious.

We got back together on Valentine's Day, and everything felt like a dream—roses, laughter, and beautiful moments filled our time together. His home came alive with our laughter during movie nights, cooking together, mixing our favorite cocktails, and playful banter. It felt like I was finally getting the reassurance for which I had longed. We settled into a comfortable rhythm, with Rob checking in throughout the day, sharing stories about his work at his engineering firm.

He often talked about his projects, showing me blueprints and explaining the details. Rob's meticulousness and perfectionism were evident in everything he did, and I admired his dedication and intellect—it was deeply attractive. He was everything I envisioned in a partner: successful, intelligent, and composed. However, I could not help but notice how different we were. Rob was calculated and precise—traits that probably came from his engineering background—whereas I was more of a free spirit, thriving on spontaneity and enjoying life in the moment.

This contrast even showed in the smallest things. When we packed for a trip, his clothes were perfectly folded and organized. I, on the other hand, was far less systematic, preferring to pack as I went along the flow during travels. I once offered to help him fold his shirts, and he gently corrected me, showing me his "system." I laughed it off, joking that I was "domestically challenged," which he found amusing. He teased that it was because I had always been focused on my career and had not been taught the "domestic arts" like his mom, a lifelong homemaker.

Despite these playful moments, I often felt like I was walking on eggshells around Rob. I could not always be myself or do things my way without feeling judged. Even when he framed our differences as complementary, saying they were what made us work as a couple, I could not shake the sense that he preferred things done his way. Still, his words gave me hope. I appreciated that he was beginning to see potential in our relationship.

Things reached a new level when Rob invited me to join his parents for his mom's birthday dinner. I was thrilled and nervous beyond belief—meeting his parents felt like a significant step. We dined at an elegant oceanfront restaurant in Newport Beach, and the evening could not have gone better. His mom was warm and welcoming, even complimenting how pretty I looked. We shared escargot, red wine martinis, laughter, and lively conversation. For the first time, I felt like I truly belonged in Rob's world.

Rob was the family's golden child, their pride and joy, and being included in such an intimate setting gave me hope. I started to believe that my doubts and insecurities had been misplaced, that all my fears about our relationship were simply impatience on my part. Meeting his parents felt like a turning point, a sign that things were finally aligning and that we were meant to be.

With renewed confidence, I allowed myself to believe that our relationship was on solid ground. What could go wrong now?

Reflection & Analysis: Dancing on Shaky Ground: Balancing Hope and Insecurity in the Quest for Belonging

While Kellie feels elated by Rob's increased consistency and gestures of commitment—such as frequent interactions, shared moments, and the pivotal introduction to his parents—there is a lingering sense of insecurity and doubt. This subtle tension stems from Kellie's awareness of their differences, moments of self-doubt, and the need to adjust to Rob's meticulous and controlling tendencies.

Kellie focuses on the positive developments, convincing herself that patience and perseverance are paying off. However, the mood is tinged with vulnerability, as she remains unsure of Rob's true feelings and struggles to balance her individuality within the relationship. The passage oscillates between joy and anxiety, reflecting the emotional highs of feeling included and the lows of self-doubt and the fear of misjudgment.

This passage reveals Kellie's emotional journey of hope and longing for validation in their relationship with Rob. It highlights a period of perceived progress, where Rob's increased consistency and gestures, such as introducing Kellie to his parents, create a sense of optimism and reassurance. However, this optimism is layered with subtle signs of tension and self-doubt, suggesting that Kellie is compromising parts of herself to align with Rob's expectations.

Kellie's admiration for Rob's qualities, like his intellect and meticulous nature, contrasts with her own free-spirited disposition, which she seems to suppress to fit into his structured world. Instances like folding clothes or adjusting to his preferences underscore an imbalance in the relationship, where Kellie feels judged and constrained. Despite Rob's suggestion that their differences could complement each other, Kellie is left feeling as though she is walking on eggshells, constantly seeking approval.

The dinner with Rob's parents serves as a climactic moment that fuels Kellie's hopes for the relationship's future. Yet, the emphasis on Rob being the "family gem" and Kellie's belief that everything is falling into place signals an overreliance on external validation. This creates a fragile foundation for her happiness, tied more to Rob's actions than to her own sense of self-worth.

Kellie's journal entry reflects a poignant mix of hope, effort, and vulnerability. It underscores Kellie's deep desire for connection and belonging but also reveals the cracks in her confidence and autonomy within the relationship. This tension suggests that the fulfillment she seeks may be overshadowed by underlying power imbalances and a lack of mutual emotional security.

Journal Entry—Day 19: Mood—oscillates between despair and hope, underscoring the complexity of navigating heartbreak and personal growth.

Today I felt deeply disempowered as I found myself trapped in a relentless loop of thoughts, analyzing the situation, missing, longing, and wondering in silence. Rob hasn't reached out either, and the cyclical pattern of yearning, doubts, and fleeting hopes keeps playing in my mind. I have thought about reaching out to him, but to what end? I don't even know my intentions. Deep down, I fear it would come from a place of desperation and lead to even more hurt if he doesn't respond. The thought of his silence or rejection feels unbearable.

I am wounded and know I need to turn my attention elsewhere. But what could Rob even offer me now? I have emotionally over-invested myself in this relationship and, in doing so, lost parts of who I am. I need time to heal, to look inward, to face my insecurities, attachment issues, and fears of abandonment. Oh my, tears are welling up again as I realize how much I've overlooked myself. The root of this pain lies in a lack of self-love. If I genuinely loved myself, I wouldn't have allowed the disrespect and emotional imbalance to continue time and time again.

But what exactly is *self-love*? I take care of myself physically, indulge in hobbies, and spend money on vanity, yet I still feel empty.

I've sought validation from others, from men like Rob, to fill the void. Why did I pour so much of myself into someone who clearly did not care for me as deeply as I cared for him? It's as though I tied my worth to how Rob saw me, romanticizing the relationship and setting unrealistic expectations without establishing firm boundaries for how I deserve to be treated.

Today, I feel an urgency to look inward and understand the vulnerability that led me here. My life was full before Rob entered the picture. I must stop fantasizing about who I thought Rob could be and let go of the idealized version of our relationship. These thoughts are overwhelming, but they are necessary. Now, I see that I, too, needed space to detach, to redirect my energy, and to focus on things that do not revolve around him.

I must release the grip I've held on this relationship, surrender the obsessive need to control its outcome, and stop forcing something that was never meant to work. It's time to let go, even in silence, because the weight of Rob and the illusion of "us" is too much to bear.

This is my moment to heal, to reclaim my power, and to take back control of my life.

Reflection & Analysis: Surrender in Silence: From Attachment to Self-Reclamation

This passage captures Kellie's struggle between lingering attachment and the dawning realization of the need for self-healing. It reflects a poignant mix of vulnerability, self-awareness, and the desire to reclaim inner strength. The emotions oscillate between yearning for Rob and recognizing the toxic cycle of overinvestment and self-abandonment. Kellie is at a crossroads, grappling with her deep emotional wounds and the longing for validation that kept her tethered to a relationship that did not nurture her.

Kellie's questioning of her intentions to reach out to Rob highlights her internal conflict—wanting connection yet fearing rejection or further pain. The admission of having "over-invested" in the relationship and "lost herself in the process" is a powerful moment of clarity. It suggests a shift from seeking external validation to confronting her own insecurities and attachment patterns.

The mood of this passage is introspective and melancholic, marked by a sense of emotional turmoil and yearning. It conveys a deep sadness and longing as Kellie grapples with feelings of loss, self-doubt, and unfulfilled expectations in the aftermath of a relationship. However, amidst the pain, there is also a sense of self-awareness and determination, as she begins to confront her vulnerabilities, reflect on the need for self-love, and resolve to heal and reclaim her autonomy.

The exploration of self-love is particularly striking. Kellie reflects on how material self-care—spending on hobbies or vanity—has not filled the emotional void. This acknowledgment underscores the complexity of self-love, which requires *emotional boundaries, self-respect, and a powerful sense of worth* independent of external validation. Kellie's insight into how she tied her value to how Rob saw her reveals an unhealthy dynamic, one that she is beginning to challenge.

The determination to detach and redirect her energy inward is a hopeful turn in the narrative. By identifying the need to "stop forcing something that never works" and let go of romanticized expectations, Kellie begins the process of reclaiming her power. The desire to "surrender in silence" reflects not defeat but a step toward healing—a willingness to face the discomfort of loss to find peace.

Kellie's journal entry captures the painful yet transformative process of disentangling from a relationship that has consumed one's sense of self. It is a raw and introspective exploration of heartbreak resilience, and the first steps toward self-reclamation.

Journal Entry—Day 20: Mood—hopeful and introspective, tinged with a sense of determination.

Today marks the first day I have summoned the courage to look inward and begin rewriting my story. I am determined to embark on a journey of self-love, though I am not entirely clear on what that entails. I once believed that treating myself to nice things meant I loved myself, yet this persistent void and emptiness tell me otherwise. Despite a successful career and the means to acquire comfort, I am confronted with the reality of my unhappiness. Why have I placed my sense of fulfillment in the hands of someone else and why have I not seen the value on things and accomplishments I have acquired?

The past few weeks have left me emotionally drained, consumed by overthinking and yearning for a man who did not choose me. I recognize now that the fleeting joy from material things does not fill the deeper void within.

Reflecting on my behavior, I see patterns that contributed to tolerating Rob's disrespect and mistreatment. If I am unhappy with where I am today, I must change the habits and thought processes that brought me here. I was not clear about what I wanted from Rob or the relationship; I allowed mistreatment and failed to stand up for my needs; my chronic insecurity made me overly dependent on external validation; I tied my value to Rob's actions and approval, leading to self-devaluation and desperation.

I can see now how Rob's push-and-pull behavior triggered my vulnerabilities. He sensed my insecurities and used them to maintain control, but if he truly cared about me, there would be no games. A loving partner would not have *left me questioning my worth*. The realization that I overinvested in someone who did not match my commitment is painful, but it's also liberating—I see where I need to grow.

It's overwhelming to think of big goals right now, so I'll focus on small, meaningful steps to regain my strength and independence. My friend's wedding in Texas is in two weeks, and I want to show up feeling grounded and composed.

For now, I will shift my focus to physical health and creating new routines. Small, achievable actions will hopefully guide me forward. I'll begin with a one-week yoga challenge at CorePower Yoga. Sculpt yoga will not only distract me but also help me release tension and grow stronger; I will focus on nourishing my body with better food choices; silence my phone, reduce mental clutter, and get adequate sleep.

Today, I commit to showing up for myself—one small step at a time. This is not about perfection or rushing the process; it's about finding a path to healing and rediscovering the parts of me I lost along the way. For now, I will focus on this first step: showing up to yoga, taking a deep breath, and starting anew.

Reflection & Analysis: From Co-Dependence to Self-Reclamation

Kellie is now beginning to demonstrate a shift from emotional turmoil to introspection and initiative-taking change. It captures a profound realization about the importance of self-love, boundaries, and in-dependence, juxtaposed with the lingering effects of heartbreak and co-dependence.

Kellie's journey is rooted in the acknowledgment of past mistakes, such as tolerating disrespect, seeking external validation, and failing to set boundaries. These admissions are honest and raw, indicating a willingness to confront uncomfortable truths. The reflection on how material possessions or professional achievements failed to fill an emotional void highlights a deeper yearning for *intrinsic* self-worth and fulfillment. This vulnerability shows a profound level of self-ex-ploration and the beginning of genuine emotional healing.

The passage explores the difference between superficial acts of self-love (treating oneself to nice things) and the deeper, more mean-ingful journey of cultivating inner peace and self-acceptance. Kellie begins to understand that true happiness cannot be found through external sources, whether people or possessions—but must come from within. It reflects the process of converting emotional pain into mo-tivation for self-improvement.

By identifying destructive habits and recognizing the patterns that led to her current state, Kellie outlines tangible steps for moving for-ward, such as focusing on health, building routines, and fostering personal growth through new hobbies like yoga. Despite lingering feelings of sadness and rejection, Kellie's tone shifts toward one of empowerment.

Phrases like "I will start today" and "one day at a time" indicate a resolve to take control of her life and break free from old cycles. This determination signifies a reclaiming of agency, even if the path ahead feels daunting. The passage captures the complexity of healing. While Kellie is hopeful, there are lingering traces of insecurity and the pain of unmet expectations. This duality reflects the realistic ebb and flow of personal growth, where progress is often accompanied by moments of doubt and struggle.

This journal entry serves as a compelling narrative of self-realization and transformation. It underscores the importance of confronting emotional wounds, learning from past mistakes, and taking deliberate steps toward self-reliance. Kellie's resolve to rebuild her sense of self and find joy independent of external validation is a testament to the resilience of the human spirit. This moment of clarity and action lays the foundation for a journey of healing and self-discovery.

Journal Entry—Day 21: Mood—resilient and introspective with undertones of determination and self-empowerment.

Yesterday, I felt proud of myself for taking action. I doubled yoga classes because my mind was consumed by thoughts of where the silence from Rob might lead. As I pushed through the discomfort of sweating and working out, I realized I was learning to sit with pain—both physical and emotional—just as I am learning to endure the breakup.

There were moments during the class when I wanted to quit, overwhelmed by lingering emotions from the breakup and the strain of physical exertion. I noticed how weak my endurance was, which only fueled my determination to grow stronger.

I felt out of place in the yoga studio, surrounded by people who seemed fit, confident, and synchronized with the flow, while I struggled to keep up with the poses. I could not ignore my physical insecurities, knowing I needed to lose weight and build strength. Still, I pushed through until the pain began to ease, and the relentless chatter in my mind finally quieted.

Afterward, I came home exhausted, my body sore from the intensity of the workout. But something felt different. For the first time in a while, I did not find myself obsessing over a text that will never come. I began to accept the reality that Rob had moved on. Instead of spiraling into overthinking, I consciously shifted my focus back to myself.

I've realized I haven't given myself enough credit for sticking to my plans and taking steps to regain control. In doing so, I felt a small but significant sense of empowerment. I haven't argued, reacted, chased, begged, pleaded or let my emotions dictate my actions to Rob. My silence somehow feels like strength, and I have no regret on how I've handled the breakup.

I am now learning to redirect the focus back to myself by acknowledging that this moment is not about Rob—it is *about me*. I am confronting my issues head-on and finding ways to reclaim my sense of self. For the time being, my priority is completing my one-week yoga challenge—to stay consistent and show up for myself, not only for my physical health but to build that muscle of confidence and discipline to move forward. One day at a time, I am starting to create a *better foundation* for myself.

Reflection & Analysis: Healing Through Discomfort

While Kellie acknowledges feelings of insecurity, emotional exhaustion, and lingering pain from the breakup, there is a noticeable shift toward hope and progress. The effort to confront and overcome personal struggles reflects a growing sense of strength and purpose. Kellie begins to focus on setting goals, achieving small victories, and finding balance highlights a mood of renewal and self-discovery, despite the challenges.

This passage reflects a profound shift toward self-empowerment and growth through self-discipline, reflection, and the pursuit of personal goals. It demonstrates Kellie's ongoing struggle with emotional pain and self-doubt but also highlights her determination to reclaim control over her life and break free from unhealthy patterns.

Kellie's effort to engage in physical activity, despite the emotional and physical discomfort, symbolizes a willingness to confront pain rather than avoid it. Yoga and exercise serve as both literal and metaphorical tools for building endurance, not only physical stamina but also emotional resilience. By enduring the immediate challenge of the workout, Kellie draws parallels to enduring the discomfort of heartbreak and the process of moving on. This alignment between physical exertion and emotional growth is a powerful metaphor for healing.

Kellie's acknowledgment of the physical and emotional challenges of her yoga practice reveals a broader truth: growth often comes through discomfort. By continuing despite feelings of inadequacy or physical pain, she demonstrates the value of persistence, even when progress feels slow or unremarkable.

As the mind quiets during the workout, Kellie experiences a reprieve from obsessive thoughts about Rob. This moment of mental clarity shows the potential of mindfulness and physical exertion to redirect focus and achieve a sense of inner peace.

Kellie reframes her silence in the aftermath of the breakup as an act of power rather than passivity. By choosing not to reach out or react, she maintains a sense of dignity and control, reclaiming emotional space to focus on her needs rather than her ex-partner's absence.

Despite moments of empowerment, Kellie grapples with feelings of inadequacy, such as not feeling "fit" enough to belong in the yoga studio. However, she counters this with determination, setting small but meaningful goals, like a one-week fitness challenge, to build confidence and achieve incremental growth.

The passage highlights Kellie's intent to shift focus from external validation (e.g., Rob's approval) to internal validation, achieved through setting and meeting personal goals. This transformation reflects a growing understanding of self-worth as something cultivated from within rather than granted by others.

Kellie is taking deliberate steps to rebuild her life after a breakup by focusing on self-improvement and emotional growth. Her journal entry is an inspiring account of someone learning to sit with discomfort, facing her vulnerabilities, and channeling her energy into positive action. While the journey is still unfolding, Kellie's determination to remain consistent and prioritize herself is a testament to her inner strength and the beginning of profound healing.

Journal Entry Day 22: Mood~Resilient and Introspective with Understones of Determiantion and Self-empowerment.

Day 2/7 yoga fitness challenge, and the physical pain from muscle soreness is beginning to outweigh the emotional pain. Despite feeling tempted to rest today, my restless mood urged me to get moving. It is only the second day—I can't afford to skip my workout already. Scrolling through Pinterest for inspiration, I came across numerous before-and-after body transformation pictures. They motivated me, so I created boards and collages filled with images that inspire me. I even found recipes for healthy, nourishing meals to support my fitness journey.

The pull to skip today is strong—I should just stay home, rest, and binge Netflix. But no. Consistency is key, and committing to myself means showing up even when I do not feel like it. Achieving my fitness goals requires discipline, and that discipline starts today. I can't bail myself out. *Prioritizing myself* is currently non-negotiable. Yes, I am still emotionally raw from the breakup, but today I am choosing to stick to the plan. I'll book another yoga sculpt class and push myself a little further. This is for me. This is my time.

Reflection & Analysis: Reclaiming Power Through Action

While there is acknowledgment of emotional pain and physical exhaustion, the overall tone of Kellie conveys a sense of commitment to personal growth, resilience, and the decision to prioritize self-care. Kellie struggles with doubt but channels her energy into action, reflecting a mood of hope and empowerment despite the challenges.

This journal entry demonstrates a powerful reflection of her evolving relationship with self-discipline, emotional resilience, and self-care. It captures the internal tug-of-war between the temptation to give in to comfort and the desire to push forward toward self-improvement. Kellie's struggle with soreness and the lingering emotional pain of a breakup mirrors the broader human experience of confronting discomfort when striving for change. Kellie's decision to continue her fitness challenge despite physical pain and emotional exhaustion shows the importance of consistency in achieving personal goals.

The repeated resolve not to "bail out" reflects a budding recognition of her own motivation and a shift toward prioritizing self-respect over fleeting feelings.

The act of seeking inspiration through Pinterest demonstrates Kellie's effort to find external motivation to fuel her internal drive. This use of visual aids and goal-setting tools highlights a pragmatic approach to overcoming inertia, showing a balance between reflection and action. The journal entry narrative illustrates the difficulty of sitting with discomfort—both emotional and physical—and the desire to channel it into productivity. This speaks to the universal challenge of navigating restlessness after emotional upheaval and transforming it into something constructive. Kellie's journal entry suggests that action, whether physical movement or planning, is an antidote to the pain of a breakup. The focus on creating new habits and achieving body goals is symbolic Kellie's attempt to rebuild her sense of self-worth and autonomy.

Kellie's journey is not just about physical fitness but also about reclaiming control and re-centering her focus after a period of emotional disarray. By choosing discipline and action over passivity, she is actively rewriting the narrative of her breakup from one of loss to one of opportunity for growth. However, the internal struggle—marked by the temptation to rest or indulge—also underscores the fragility of this newfound resolve, suggesting that true transformation requires persistence and self-compassion. Overall, the passage captures the resilience and determination required to break free from old patterns and invest in self-love, portraying a relatable and inspiring story of personal empowerment.

Journal Entry—Day 23: Mood—hopeful and determined.

Day 3/7 yoga fitness challenge feels like a turning point. I am committed to attending another class after work, and the act of booking it solidifies my intention. I spent some time pinning healthy and delicious recipes to try, sparking excitement for nourishing my body in alignment with my goals. A trip to Whole Foods is on my agenda to gather the ingredients I need, adding a layer of purpose to my day as I invest in my well-being.

Today, I feel a sense of alignment, mentally and physically. The momentum is building, and with my friend's wedding around the corner, I am motivated by the thought of looking and feeling great in an outfit that reflects my progress. While my focus is on small daily steps, the energy I feel today reminds me that this is about more than just the wedding. It's about becoming a better, stronger version of myself.

I am halfway through my one-week challenge, and while I don't yet know what comes next, I've learned to embrace the process one day at a time. I am also mindful of not overwhelming myself with overly ambitious goals. Consistency is key, and today, it feels good to balance effort with self-compassion. With renewed energy, I have committed to another yoga sculpt class, reminding myself that each step forward is a victory.

Reflection & Analysis: Small Steps Big Impact

Kellie conveys a sense of renewed energy and optimism as Kellie embraces her fitness challenge and personal growth journey. There is an underlying tone of self-discipline and pride in taking consistent, meaningful steps toward self-improvement. While the passage acknowledges lingering uncertainties, it is balanced by a positive outlook, focusing on small victories and a forward-thinking mindset.

This journal entry reflects a pivotal moment of self-empowerment and progress, highlighting Kellie's commitment to personal growth and the pursuit of well-being. The entry highlights a transition from emotional turbulence to a more grounded and purposeful mindset. By setting achievable goals and focusing on incremental progress, Kellie demonstrates resilience and determination to build a healthier relationship with herself.

Kellie is actively working to redirect her energy from past emotional pain toward self-care and self-improvement. She recognizes the value of small, consistent steps and the importance of committing to herself—a significant shift from previous patterns of seeking external validation. Her sense of purpose is fueled by a tangible goal, such as preparing for her friend's wedding, but the deeper significance lies in cultivating self-respect and personal accountability.

Kellie acknowledges her incremental achievements (day 3 of the challenge, feeling more energy, committing to yoga), which reinforces her sense of accomplishment and builds momentum. She recognizes the temptation to overextend herself but consciously chooses to focus on manageable, daily goals. This approach reflects self-awareness and a commitment to *sustainable change*. By establishing *routines* like meal planning, grocery shopping, and yoga, Kellie creates a framework for stability. These habits not only serve her fitness goals but also promote a sense of control over her life.

While Kellie is still in the process of healing, the tone reflects a growing confidence in her ability to move forward. The shift from emotional focus to action-oriented thinking represents progress. Overall, the journal entry serves as a powerful testament to Kellie's determination to reclaim her sense of identity and purpose. It reflects both the challenges and triumphs of self-healing, emphasizing the transformative potential of consistent, intentional action.

Journal Entry—Day 24: Mood—determined and hopeful, with an underlying sense of empowerment and self-awareness.

I did a grocery haul filled with healthy foods and, for the first time, I'm trying my hand at meal prepping. I've decided to commit to a high-protein, high-fiber diet rich in vegetables and other nourishing foods. Day 4/7 of my fitness goal challenge feels like I've truly embraced this new journey—my energy levels are noticeably improving, and it might be because I've shifted my focus away from lamenting about Rob. Diet planning and exercise have become anchors for my mind, keeping me busy and providing a release for the tension and anxiety I have been carrying since the breakup.

Today, I am setting intentional goals to fully commit to this transformation journey. While it is still early, I feel determined to prove to myself that I can stick to this plan. I want to prioritize myself, even though I'm still hurting. Diverting all that attention and energy I used to give to Rob—and our relationship—toward my own growth feels like the right path forward.

Looking back, I realize how much I neglected myself by putting my own needs last. I became so consumed with the outcome of our relationship and so over-invested that I lost sight of the simple joys of self-care. This time, I'm changing that. I need to heal my wounded heart, rebuild my self-esteem, and regain my confidence. Taking control of my health and fitness feels incredibly empowering, it is something I can own and direct. While I can no longer control what happened with Rob or the outcome of our relationship, I can control what I eat and how I commit to my fitness routine.

Today, I am choosing to focus on the things I can control.

Reflection & Analysis: From Heartbreak to Self-Care

Kellie acknowledges the lingering pain and emotional challenges from her breakup, but her focus has shifted toward personal growth and regaining control over her life. While there are traces of introspection and vulnerability, her overall tone is one of optimism and resilience as she channels her energy into her health, fitness, and self-care.

Kellie's journal entry reflects a significant turning point in her personal journey, characterized by self-awareness, determination, and a renewed commitment to self-care. Kellie openly recognizes how she prioritized her relationship with Rob to the detriment of her own needs. This introspection shows emotional growth and an under-standing of how overinvestment and neglecting self-care contributed to her current emotional state. She is redirecting her energy from lamenting over her breakup to tangible actions that prioritize her well-being. By meal prepping and committing to a fitness routine, Kellie demonstrates a proactive approach to healing and self-improve-ment.

Kellie identifies that while she cannot control the outcome of her relationship, she can control her health and fitness. This realization symbolizes reclaiming agency and shifting her mindset from one loss to one of empowerment. While she acknowledges that her journey is just beginning, her commitment to staying consistent with her goals reveals a budding sense of optimism and belief in her ability to trans-form herself.

The entry shows Kellie's ability to process her emotions construc-tively. Rather than being consumed by pain, she channels her feel-ings into actionable steps, a hallmark of emotional resilience. Kellie's recognition of her role in the relationship dynamic and her decision to change habits reflects maturity and a willingness to take accountabil-ity. This self-awareness is pivotal for long-term growth and healing. By focusing on her health and fitness, Kellie is not only addressing physical well-being but also rebuilding her confidence and self-es-teem. These actions signify a deeper commitment to herself beyond external validation. The act of meal prepping, exercising, and setting intentional goals serves as a healthy distraction and coping mechanism. Instead of seeking solace in self-destructive behaviors, she is choosing activities that promote growth and stability.

Kellie's journal entry encapsulates a pivotal moment of transfor-mation. Her ability to reflect on her past, acknowledge her pain, and channel her energy into self-improvement signifies a transition from vulnerability to strength. This is not just about fitness or diet but about reclaiming her identity, healing her emotional wounds, and rediscovering her worth. While the journey is still early, her determination and focus suggest that she is on a promising path toward empowerment and personal fulfillment.

Journal Entry Day 25: Mood ~ Reflective and Resolute, with undertones of Emotional Pain and Growing Empowerment.

The lingering thoughts of the breakup and the emotional triggers still surface, and the deafening silence of no contact weighs heavily on me. I find myself wondering what has become of us. Yet, amidst the noise of my constant mind chatter, yoga offers a temporary reprieve. In the heat of summer, I step into a room filled with people practicing hot yoga. The discomfort is almost unbearable, but it's becoming familiar, teaching me to sit with unease and embrace it rather than resist.

As I move through the asanas, the chaos in my mind gives way to stillness. My attention is pulled inward as each pose demands focus on my body's sensations and my breath aligns with movement. Sweat drips, the heat intensifies, and every ounce of my energy is poured into my breathing. For once, the thoughts of Rob and the heartbreak quiet, replaced by an awareness of the life force within a humbling reminder of my resilience.

In this space, I find a glimmer of hope that things will get better. The breathing soothes my aching heart, which had been yearning for something I thought was love. In the struggle, I discover strength. Unlike before, when I would numb the pain through rebounds, alcohol, impulsive spending, or other distractions, I now feel an urge to confront the pain directly. I want to understand its roots and fill the void from within, without seeking external validation.

This silence is a gift, allowing me to reevaluate my life and emotions. Moving my body through yoga has become an elixir for my grief, grounding me in the present and soothing my mind. It is painful to face the truth: Rob's lack of care and abrupt departure reflects his disregard for me. Someone who genuinely cares do not just leave without explanation or compassion. I see now that I was used, and while the realization stings, it is giving me clarity to move forward.

Reflection & Analysis: In The Quiet, I Heal

Kellie's journal entry reflects a profound emotional and mental shift, displaying her journey toward understanding and healing through the pain of her breakup. While she acknowledges the lingering sadness, heartache, and betrayal from her breakup, there is also a sense of determination and focus on healing. Her mood evolves as she finds solace in the process of moving her body through yoga and confronting her feelings, shifting toward clarity, acceptance, and a budding hope for self-renewal.

The interplay between vulnerability and strength defines her mood, as she navigates through the discomfort with grace and begins to reclaim her power. There is an air of quiet resolve and self-discovery as she commits to prioritizing her well-being and rebuilding her confidence.

Kellie's journal entry is a testament to her emotional strength and commitment to self-improvement. While the heartbreak remains fresh, the act of embracing discomfort and finding solace in yoga indicates a significant shift in perspective. By acknowledging the truth of the relationship and turning inward, she is reclaiming her narrative and paving the way for healing, self-love, and empowerment.

The entry captures the raw, unfiltered emotions surrounding the breakup, including the ache of rejection and the torment of unanswered questions. However, there is a noticeable shift from being overwhelmed by these feelings to processing them constructively.

One of the most striking aspects of this entry is Kellie's ability to embrace discomfort—both physical and emotional. Yoga serves as a metaphor for life's challenges, teaching Kellie to sit in pain rather than avoid it. This symbolizes growth and resilience.

The focus on yoga highlights the therapeutic power of movement and mindfulness. As Kellie synchronizes breath with movement, she creates space for healing and self-awareness. The act of turning inward contrasts with past habits of externalizing or numbing pain.

The absence of noise, both literal and metaphorical, gives Kellie the clarity to understand her emotions and the dynamics of the relationship. The realization that Rob lacked care and respect is painful but empowering, as it helps shift blame away from herself. Accepting the truth of Rob's behavior—while difficult—is a step toward reclaiming Kellie's power.

The entry demonstrates Kellie's resolve to prioritize self-understanding and self-worth rather than dwelling on someone who did not value her. Kellie's journey is one of the transformations, marked by a determination to change old patterns. The decision to face pain head-on, rather than seeking distractions, reflects maturity and a desire for lasting growth.

Journal Entry Day 26: Mood~ Hopeful and Empowered, with an Undertone of Reflection and Guarded Vulnerability.

Today, for the first time in a while, I felt like myself again—a sense of renewal and mental clarity has begun to take hold. After my yoga class, I felt motivated to embrace the warm summer day. I decided to take my dog, Bailey, to Huntington Dog Beach. I realized how little attention I have given him during the emotional turmoil of my breakup.

While I've kept up with feeding and walking him, I haven't truly taken the time to play or enjoy his company. The weight of my own healing had consumed me, leaving me feeling guilty for neglecting one of the few sources of unconditional love in my life. Determining to change that, I packed up and took Bailey to the beach. Watching him joyfully fetch the ball I tossed, feeling the cool ocean breeze against my skin, and gazing at the vast open sea filled me with a sense of lightness and hope.

The beach, with its calming rhythm of waves, reminded me of better days to come. I felt a renewed strength, both physically and mentally—a byproduct of weeks of consistent exercise and pushing myself in yoga and sculpt classes.

In those classes, the intense physical effort often feels like a release, counterbalancing or even overpowering the emotional pain of my breakup. Staying active has been my solace, silencing the overthinking that used to overwhelm me. I find myself grateful for the peace these routines bring.

Today, I also reflected on my journey of maintaining no contact with Rob. While the temptation to reach out sometimes lingers, especially in moments of yearning, I am proud that I have not given in. Rob has not reached out either, or though the silence is difficult, I recognize it as essential for my healing. I know that if he contacted me, I might falter emotionally—I am still vulnerable. For now, this quiet distance is helping me see things more clearly.

I am beginning to understand the reality of our relationship and Rob's lack thereof. Though the pain is still present, my silence is saving me. I have found strength in honoring myself, in staying committed to my healing, and in seeking joy from within rather than from him. Today felt like a step forward, a small but meaningful victory.

Reflection & Analysis: The Quiet Rebirth

Kellie expresses a sense of renewal and clarity as she takes pro-active steps to reconnect with herself and find joy in simple pleasures like playing with her dog, Bailey, and embracing the warm summer day. Her newfound motivation for physical activity and the strength she is gaining from maintaining no contact with Rob reveal a growing sense of self-reliance and determination. While she still acknowledges lingering emotional pain and moments of temptation to reach out, she is proud of her ability to resist, seeing the silence as a necessary part of her healing.

Kellie feels a balance between her emotional struggles and the em-powerment that comes from focusing on herself, setting boundaries, and staying committed to her growth. Kellie's journal entry reflects a significant turning point in her healing journey. It portrays her growing ability to navigate emotional pain with resilience, redirecting her energy toward self-care and moments of genuine connection with her environment. She acknowledges how her emotional turmoil has affected her daily life, including her interactions with her dog, Bailey. Her recognition of neglecting the small joys—like playing with her dog—highlights a deepening sense of self-awareness.

By reflecting on this, she acknowledges the disruptive impact of the breakup and the emotional toll it has taken. Importantly, she does not dwell solely on regret but uses this realization as a springboard to reconnect with what matters to her. Physical activity, particularly yoga and sculpt classes, serves as both a metaphor and a literal tool for Kellie's healing. She finds solace in the intensity of physical exertion, which mirrors her emotional pain and provides a cathartic release. This routine helps her silence her overthinking mind and fosters a sense of control over her life. The juxtaposition of physical strength with emotional vulnerability demonstrates her commitment to holistic healing.

Kellie reveals the strength she is gaining by maintaining no contact with Rob. While she still battles the impulse to reach out, her resolve to prioritize her healing over seeking answers or closure reflects emotional growth. She recognizes that any contact might reopen wounds and derail her progress, showing that she is developing healthy boundaries for herself.

Despite the lingering sadness, Kellie's ability to appreciate small moments of joy—such as playing fetch with Bailey or feeling the ocean breeze—suggests a rekindling of hope. Her statement about silence "saving her" encapsulates the empowerment she derives from choosing herself over emotional reactivity. This empowerment is further reinforced by her focus on self-improvement, both physically and emotionally.

While Kellie demonstrates growth, she is still processing the emotional impact of the breakup. Her reflection on Rob's absence and her resentment towards him for causing emotional disruption indicates unresolved feelings. However, instead of being consumed by these emotions, she channels them into constructive actions like exercise and self-reflection, showing she is learning to sit with discomfort rather than avoiding it.

Kellie's journal entry is a testament to the transformative power of intentional self-care and personal accountability. Her journey underscores the importance of creating space to process emotions, setting boundaries, and focusing on what can be controlled. While healing remains a work in progress, her ability to balance vulnerability with resilience signifies meaningful progress toward emotional recovery and self-reclamation.

Journal Entry—Day 27: Mood—reflective, empowered, and content.

Today, I did a Costco haul to prep healthy meals. I picked up ground turkey, sockeye salmon, egg whites, greens, veggies, fruits, almond milk, and vitamin supplements. I've found meal prepping enjoyable—it's become something I truly look forward to. Cooking at home feels satisfying, and I've shifted away from eating out. As I've become more physically active, I've also become more mindful about what I eat. A high-protein diet is fueling my energy and meeting the demands of my workouts.

I find small joys in blending smoothies with fruits, nuts, blueberries, bananas, and protein or collagen powder. It is refreshing to be so intentional about taking care of myself. Why hadn't I done this before? While I have taken care of myself in the past, this time feels different—I'm consistent, and I can already feel the positive impact of clean eating and regular exercise.

This seven-day Yoga challenge is something that got me started to, is something I would continue to sustain. Yoga is becoming an elixir to my pain in a really good way. Every time I hit the mat; it is a choice that I consciously make that prioritizes my well-being.

I have also realized that I haven't had a single drink of alcohol for almost a month now. What used to be a habit—drinking a glass or two of wine every night—has been replaced with nourishing smoothies and healthy dinners to prepare my body for the next day's workout. These small but significant changes reflect a shift in how I prioritize my well-being.

On another note, I've started embracing my natural self. For years, I have straightened my hair both chemically and with heat tools. Now, I have decided to let my natural curls shine. I've also removed the acrylics from my nails, giving them a break and letting them grow naturally. I feel lighter, less constrained, and more at peace.

There's a renewed focus on prioritizing myself and my health. This shift has been about finding joy in activities that please me, rather than striving to please others. I'm setting personal goals and achieving them for my own sense of fulfillment, not anyone else's expectations. It feels empowering to center my attention on my own growth, peace, and happiness.

Reflection & Analysis: Reclaiming My True Self

Kellie's mood exhibits a sense of self-awareness and gratitude for the positive changes she is making in her life. Her focus on healthy habits, self-care, and personal growth gives her a feeling of renewal and ac-complishment. There's also an underlying sense of calm and confidence as she embraces her natural self as she lets go of old habits and prioritizes her own needs. While the entry reflects introspection about past behaviors, the overall tone is one of optimism and empowerment, as she feels in control of her journey and is finding joy in nurturing herself.

Kellie's journal entry reflects a significant shift in her mindset and approach to life, showcasing a deliberate effort to prioritize her health, self-care, and well-being. Kellie's journey highlights a profound transformation, both physically and emotionally. By committing to meal prepping, clean eating, and embracing her natural beauty, she is reclaiming autonomy over her life. These changes symbolize her desire to strip away external pressures and return to her authentic self. This shift underscores a theme of renewal—she is letting go of past habits and patterns that no longer serve her.

Her focus on preparing nutritious meals, embracing her natural curls, and discontinuing the use of acrylic nails reveals a deeper connection with self-acceptance. These acts of self-care are not superficial; they represent a reclaiming of her identity and values. She is finding joy in nurturing herself and feels more in tune with her body and mind. This empowerment stems from creating a lifestyle that prioritizes her needs rather than seeking validation from external sources.

Kellie contrasts her newfound habits with past behaviors, such as drinking wine as a coping mechanism or prioritizing others over herself. Her reflection conveys a sense of liberation from these old patterns. The decision to replace wine with smoothies and focus on activities that align with her health goals symbolizes her growing emotional resilience and ability to confront challenges constructively.

Kellie's mindfulness is evident as she notes the small joys of her routine, such as blending smoothies or preparing meals. She expresses gratitude for how these practices are positively impacting her energy and mindset. This mindfulness extends to her emotional growth; she recognizes how focusing on herself instead of pleasing others has led to a shift in her priorities and overall happiness. While acknowledging that this is part of a journey, Kellie emphasizes her consistency and commitment to her goals. She sees these small but steady steps as building blocks for long-term growth. Her tone reflects a sense of pride in the progress she has made and optimism for the future.

Kellie's journal entry is a testament to the power of intentional living. By turning inward and dedicating herself to self-care, she has found a way to balance her emotional healing with actionable goals. This process not only helps her manage the aftermath of emotional challenges of the breakup but also positions her for a more fulfilling and centered life. Her journey is a reminder that personal transformation often begins with small, deliberate choices that align with one's core values and priorities.

Journal Entry—Day 28: Mood—conflicted yet introspective, evolving toward empowerment and gratitude.

Today, I embarked on a road trip for a weekend getaway with my girlfriends. It is a tradition for the seven of us to escape to Palm Desert each summer for some fun in the sun, dining, and a night out. My friend, Krisi, owns a vacation house there, and despite our busy lives, we have managed to keep this tradition alive over the years. Most of my friends are married, leaving me as the only single one. They leave their husbands behind for the weekend, and we savor this time to reconnect and enjoy each other's company.

While I cherish my independence as a single woman, I also long for partnership and romantic connection. My recent relationship with Rob was one I considered deeply meaningful and serious. I had genuine hopes for us, so the breakup still weighs heavily on me. During the four-hour drive, my mind wandered back to him. A strong urge welled up in me to reach out, to bridge the silence that's been deafening.

In the past, I would update Rob on my whereabouts, sending him pictures, sharing my adventures, and staying connected. I caught myself wanting to text him, something simple like, "Hi," or "How have you been?" I imagined telling him about the road trip and the weekend plans. The impulse was intense, fueled by the highway's monotony and a deep-seated yearning for validation. I convinced myself I could oversee reconnecting now that I have been focused on healing and taking care of myself. I thought I'd grown strong enough for casual communication.

But I paused. Would reaching out truly serve me? Would it honor the progress I have made? I have been diligent about healing, working to rebuild my sense of self-worth. Would texting Rob undo that progress, throwing away my dignity for a fleeting moment of connection?

I wrestled with these questions, overwhelmed by emotions. What were my intentions? Did I genuinely want to reconnect, or was I seeking attention from someone who hurt me? As I interrogated my motives, the truth stung: I still felt unworthy, still sought external validation, even from someone who lacked the intentions I deserved.

Tears fell as I grappled with the void Rob left behind. Why couldn't I simply enjoy this moment? I was on my way to a weekend with friends who love and care for me. Why couldn't that be enough? Frustration bubbled up as I questioned my attachment to him and my inability to embrace the privilege of this trip wholeheartedly.

Then, a pivotal realization dawned: I need to cultivate my own sense of worth and joy. I promised myself to stop seeking validation from others, especially Rob, and to begin celebrating my achievements and experiences on my own. This road trip is mine. These memories are mine. I want to treasure them without feeling the need to share them with anyone else's approval.

As I arrived at Palm Desert, I met my friends at a hotel bar where they were listening to jazz music. The warm summer night felt like a comforting embrace. Seeing my friends, exchanging warm hellos and hugs, filled me with relief and gratitude. I was glad I had let myself feel the full weight of my emotions during the drive and resisted the impulse to text Rob.

Silence, I have realized, is a powerful teacher. It has given me the space to process my feelings and make thoughtful choices. By choosing not to act on fear or impulsiveness, I preserved the integrity of this weekend and my own sense of progress. Breaking the silence might have jeopardized my peace—whether through rejection, reigniting old emotions, or spiraling back into despair.

Tonight, I felt a quiet triumph. The progress I am making is real, and it's rooted in putting myself first. I'm learning that I don't need anyone else to validate my journey. This trip, this time with my friends, and this celebration of independence are more than enough.

Reflection & Analysis: Navigating Longing & Embracing Self-Love

Kellie's mood in this passage is conflicted as she struggles with an intense urge to reach out to Rob, driven by a need for connection and validation. This internal conflict causes emotional turmoil, including self-doubt and frustration. Through deep reflection, she becomes acutely aware of her motivations and insecurities. She questions her intentions and recognizes patterns of seeking external affirmation.

By resisting the impulse to text Rob, Kellie asserts control over her emotions. This choice signifies her progress in prioritizing her own healing and dignity. Upon reuniting with her friends and immersing herself in the moment, she shifts to a mood of appreciation for her friendships, independence, and personal growth. Overall, her mood transitions from inner turbulence to a sense of self-assurance and gratitude for the present.

Kellie's journal entry reflects a profound journey of self-awareness, emotional resilience, and personal growth. Kellie battles a powerful impulse to reach out to Rob, driven by lingering feelings and a yearning for connection. This reflects her ongoing healing process and the challenge of breaking free from patterns of seeking external validation. The internal dialogue reveals her growing self-awareness, as she questions the intentions and consequences of acting on her impulse.

Kellie demonstrates emotional intelligence by recognizing her triggers, such as the long drive and memories of sharing updates with Rob. She allows herself to fully experience and process emotions like frustration, self-pity, and longing, rather than numbing or avoiding them. By choosing not to act on her impulse, Kellie prioritizes her self-respect and healing. Her decision marks a shift toward valuing her independence and recognizing her worth apart from Rob. She consciously challenges herself to savor moments for their own sake and to cultivate internal validation.

The trip becomes a metaphor for Kellie's journey of reclaiming her identity and joy. The companionship of her friends and the warmth of their reunion highlight the support and love she still has in her life. Her ability to focus on the present, despite emotional triggers, symbolizes her progress in building a life centered on her own happiness. Silence emerges as both a challenge and a tool for healing. By resisting the urge to text Rob, Kellie learns the value of sitting with discomfort, processing her emotions, and finding clarity in her decisions.

Kellie's journal entry is a testament to the power of self-reflection and intentional choices in the face of emotional adversity. Her journey underscores the importance of acknowledging one's emotions while consciously steering thoughts and actions toward personal growth. She is navigating the delicate balance between mourning her past relationship and embracing her future. The decision to prioritize herself, her friendships, and her independence illustrates her resilience and determination to build a life rooted in self-love and fulfillment.

By the end of the entry, Kellie demonstrates noteworthy progress in her healing journey. The clarity and peace she experienced from staying true to her commitment to herself is a powerful reminder of the rewards of patience, self-awareness, and courage in facing emotional pain head-on. Kellie's Journal Entry is a snapshot of transformation—where pain meets growth, and vulnerability gives way to strength.

Journal Entry—Day 29: Mood—calm, resilient, and self-assured, with an undercurrent of gratitude and self-awareness.

As my friends and I sat in the lounge, enjoying the live music, we caught up on each other's lives. The mood was light, filled with laughter and playful banter. Conversations flowed about their busy lives, husbands, and the daily grind of obligations. I listened intently, soaking in the moment.

Melinda turned to me and, with a warm smile, complimented me on my appearance. She asked about my workout routine, noting that

I had lost weight. She added, "You look so calm and at peace." Her words touched me deeply. If only she knew the effort, discipline, and emotional work behind that calm exterior. Beneath it all were tumultuous waves of healing and self-discovery. Still, her kind words lifted my spirit. I expressed my gratitude sincerely, sharing that I had been navigating the heartache of a breakup and staying committed to no contact.

As I disclosed my journey, my friends listened with empathy. I told them how I was learning to accept the breakup, focusing on myself, and finding the strength to move forward. Interestingly, as I spoke, I realized I no longer felt the emotional intensity that had once gripped me when mentioning Rob. What was once a raw and painful narrative now felt like a simple recounting of events. Where tears used to flow, I now found emotional control, even a sense of indifference.

Beverly expressed her sympathy, saying, "I'm so sorry it ended." To my surprise, I replied with ease, "Oh, don't be. I'm doing alright now—it's old news." I transitioned the conversation effortlessly, as though the breakup no longer weighed on me.

This silence I've chosen, this deliberate space away from contact, has become my sanctuary. It has given me the time and perspective to feel and process my emotions fully. The feelings ebb and flow, coming and going like waves. What I have discovered in this silence is a profound truth: I don't need to act on every emotion. Instead, I can sit with them, face the pain directly, and then, slowly, let it release.

Through this process, I've shed layers of self-doubt, pity, fear, and negative self-talk. In their place, I've cultivated self-compassion, forgiveness, acceptance, and a deep appreciation for my own resilience. This journey has shown me my worth and given me the confidence to trust myself.

As I reflected on Melinda's compliment, I realized that the peace she noticed was real—hard-earned and deeply transformative. I am grateful for this growing sense of calm, for the strength to trust that all will be well, and for the reassuring knowledge that I can rely on myself. That peace is becoming a part of me, and seeing it reflected in the eyes of a dear friend felt like a quiet triumph.

Reflection & Analysis: Quiet Strength

Kellie's mood in this journal entry is one of calm, resilience, and self-assurance, with an undercurrent of gratitude and self-awareness. She reflects on her growth and healing journey, acknowledging the progress she has made. While discussing her breakup, she feels a newfound emotional detachment, signaling that she is moving past the despair and heartbreak that once consumed her.

Kellie's gratitude for her friends' empathy and her ability to recognize her own inner strength show a sense of peace and self-compassion. Her mood is reflective but also hopeful, as she appreciates her personal growth and the resilience she has cultivated.

Kellie's journal entry reflects a pivotal moment in her healing journey where self-awareness and inner strength take center stage. Her recounting of the conversation with her friends, particularly Melinda's compliment, highlights the emotional and physical progress she has made since her breakup.

The entry shows her ability to recognize and articulate the hard work and discipline she has invested in her healing. Kellie describes discussing her breakup without the emotional intensity that once accompanied it. This shift indicates significant emotional growth. Where there was once despair, there is now a sense of indifference and control. This marks her transition from being consumed by her loss to becoming an observer of her experiences.

Silence emerges as a recurring theme in Kellie's reflections. She credits her decision to embrace silence with allowing her to process and release her emotions in a healthy manner. This conscious choice has enabled her to confront pain without acting impulsively, transforming self-doubt and pity into self-compassion and acceptance.

Kellie identifies her ability to navigate through tough emotions and situations as a testament to her resilience. This realization bolsters her self-worth, providing reassurance that she can rely on herself to face future challenges. Her friend Melinda's compliment serves as external validation of Kellie's internal transformation. It acts as a mirror, reflecting the calm and peace she has cultivated through consistent effort. This external acknowledgment reinforces Kellie's confidence and affirms that her hard work is not only noticed but also impactful.

Despite her focus on self-healing, Kellie remains deeply appreciative of her friends and their support. Her ability to openly share her journey with them highlights her emotional honesty and her growing sense of community, which is an integral part of her overall well-being. Kellie's journal entry is a powerful example of post-traumatic growth—how individuals can emerge from difficult experiences with a stronger sense of self and a deeper appreciation for life.

Kellie demonstrates an evolving capacity to navigate her emotions thoughtfully, using reflection as a tool for personal growth. Her acknowledgment of the fleeting nature of emotions and her practice of self-compassion signifies a mature and healthy mindset. Furthermore, the balance she strikes between independence and social connection underscores her adaptability and emotional intelligence.

Kellie's journey, as chronicled in this entry, underscores the transformative power of introspection, resilience, and self-care. She is learning to value herself and her achievements independently of external validation, signaling a shift toward a more empowered and fulfilling life. This moment of calm and self-assurance serves as a beacon of hope for her continued growth and healing.

Journal Entry—Day 30:
Mood—lighthearted, carefree, and rejuvenated.

I spent the day basking under the sun with friends at Krisi's vacation house in Palm Desert. The intense August heat was no match for our laughter and the cool relief of the pool. With margaritas in hand, we let the day unfold leisurely, dipping in and out of the water and enjoying the carefree ambiance. It felt like a welcomed indulgence, a brief departure from my usual routine of workouts and abstinence from alcohol. The sun's warmth, the soothing music in the background, and the easy chatter created a sense of dazed relaxation that I had not experienced in a long time.

As evening descended, we headed to The Nest Restaurant & Bar for dinner. The atmosphere was lively, filled with laughter and conversation as we reveled in each other's company. The night transitioned seamlessly into dancing as the live music started, drawing guests to the dance floor. For the first time in months, I found myself fully immersed in the moment. I danced, laughed, and even chatted with a couple of people who struck up conversations with me. For those hours, Rob and the pain of the breakup felt distant—like a weight I had temporarily set down.

The music, movement, and camaraderie of the evening were liberating. I let go of my overthinking and simply embraced the joy of being present. It was a night to let the fun and spontaneity of life take over, without the usual emotional undercurrent pulling me back into introspection.

As my friends and I Ubered our way back to the vacation house, I felt content. Before crashing into bed, I took a moment to reflect and write down today's memories, a spark of amusement and spirit ignited within me. This day was a much-needed escape, a reminder that I'm capable of finding joy again. With thoughts packaged neatly away, I'm ready to drift off into dreams, grateful for this lighthearted getaway.

Reflection & Analysis: Rebuilding Sense of Self & Happiness

Kellie experienced a sense of relief and joy as she allowed herself to relax, have fun, and enjoy the moment with her friends. The mood was characterized by a shift away from the emotional weight of her breakup, as she embraced the spontaneity of the day and night. Her reflection at the end suggests a mix of gratitude and hope, as she recognized her ability to find happiness and amusement despite recent emotional turmoil.

Kellie's journal entry reflects a significant emotional shift for Kellie as she steps into a space of joy, connection, and freedom. The day's activities—a mix of relaxation, socializing, and dancing—offer her a reprieve from the emotional challenges she's been navigating since her breakup. The tone of her writing suggests that she's starting to rediscover her capacity for lightheartedness and fun, underscoring her resilience and growth.

Kellie allowed herself to fully engage in the moment, immersing herself in the pleasures of companionship and celebration. This marks a shift from her previous entries, which often focused on introspection and healing. Here, she steps into a space of carefree enjoyment, signaling her ability to embrace happiness again.

The absence of thoughts about Rob during the festivities shows Kellie's growing ability to compartmentalize her emotions and enjoy the present. This detachment, even if temporary, highlights progress in her journey toward emotional independence. Her connection with her friends provided not only distraction but also a source of genuine support and joy. The shared laughter and camaraderie demonstrate the importance of her social circle in helping her heal and reconnect with herself.

The day serves as a testament to the transformative power of stepping out of one's comfort zone and engaging in activities that spark joy. Kellie's willingness to indulge in the spontaneity of dancing, socializing, and letting go of rigid routines suggests that she's balancing her disciplined healing process with moments of pure, unstructured fun.

While Kellie acknowledges the emotional turmoil of the breakup in passing, she refrains from dwelling on it. This indicates emotional growth and a developing sense of resilience. Her ability to focus on the "spark of amusement" rather than ruminate on past pain suggests that she is adapting and finding new ways to move forward. By taking the time to write about her experience, Kellie reinforces the positive aspects of the day. Her reflection shows gratitude for the moment and a recognition of her progress, which will motivate her to continue seeking and embracing joy.

Kellie's journal entry captures a turning point in her journey—where healing is no longer solely about processing pain but also about reclaiming joy and a sense of normalcy. This day serves as a reminder to her that moments of lightness and fun are possible, even amidst life's challenges. It is a small but powerful victory in her quest to rebuild her sense of self and happiness.

Journal Entry Day 31: Mood~Conflicted and Introspective, with a Strong Undercurrent of Anxiety and Disempowerment.

Last night, Rob's voice echoed hauntingly in my dream: "Kellie, have you already forgotten me?" "I just wanted to say hi." "Did you delete my number?" His presence felt oppressive, rekindling that familiar anxiety—the uncertainty of our relationship. In the dream, I was thrust back into that exhausting space of trying to prove my worth, hoping he would see me, choose me, and offer the reassurance of love and commitment I craved.

I wanted to escape, to silence the fear of losing him. But in the dream, I had nothing left to give. My voice was muted, no matter how hard I tried to respond. I wanted to tell him, "No, I didn't delete your number." "Yes, I miss you." "I've waited for you to reach out, to apologize." Yet the more I tried to speak, the quieter my voice became, until my words dissolved entirely. I was left feeling small, suffocated, and utterly powerless.

I woke up gasping for air, my chest tight and heavy, consumed by a wave of anxiety. The dream lingered, oppressive and disorienting. I blamed it partly on the alcohol from last night—a couple of margaritas after months of sobriety. My head pounded, and my body ached in a way I hadn't experienced in a long time. The familiar heaviness reminded me of the nights I drank with Rob—cranberry vodka for me, gin and tonic for him. Back then, the buzz was thrilling, but the crash that followed left me anxious and unsure, clinging to his texts for reassurance.

This morning, that old feeling resurfaced. I panicked, wondering if I'd sent him a drunk text or called him. My hands shook as I checked my phone, scrolling through my history. Relief washed over me when I found no trace of contact with Rob. But then I noticed a message from a man I had met at the bar. "Good morning, so good chatting with you last night, let me know when you are leaving town. We can get together for coffee or something." I did not even remember giving him my number. I cringed, deleted the text, and blocked his number immediately. I just did not feel ready for any type of possibility of romantic interest or interaction.

My friends woke up and suggested breakfast. I took Tylenol, gulped water, and admitted I was hungover. They reassured me that I had not drunk much, but my body was not used to alcohol anymore. I felt quiet and withdrawn, haunted by my dream and the feelings it triggered. At breakfast, I could not shake paranoia and heaviness.

The alcohol had not just upset my physical balance; it had stirred up memories and emotions I have worked so hard to heal from. That awful dream, the headache, the dehydration all reminded me why I chose sobriety and silence. I do not want to feel this way again. Suffocation, confusion, anxieties, and self-doubt; today, I am reaffirming my commitment to myself. To peace. To healing. To move forward, one step at a time in the absence of alcohol.

Reflection & Analysis: Healing Through Nightmares & Hangovers

Kellie's introspection and emotional depth intact while improving clarity and flow, captures the turmoil of the dream, the unsettling effects of alcohol, and her determination to stay on her path of healing. Waking from a nightmarish dream about Rob, she feels a mix of fear, vulnerability, and frustration, which is exacerbated by the physical effects of her hangover. Her mood shifts toward paranoia as she worries about her actions the previous night, reflecting a sense of unease and lack of control. However, amidst this turmoil, there is a spark of determination and self-awareness.

Kellie reflects deeply on her emotional triggers and reaffirms her commitment to healing and regaining her inner strength. By the end of the entry, her mood transitions toward resolve and empowerment as she chooses to prioritize her well-being over past patterns of seeking external validation.

Kellie's journal entry is a candid exploration of emotional vulnerability, self-awareness, and the ongoing struggle to reclaim personal power after a challenging breakup. The entry reflects her heightened sensitivity to her emotions, her past relationship, and her progress in healing. Kellie's dream about Rob exposes lingering fears and unresolved emotions tied to their relationship.

The dream vividly captures her sense of being voiceless and powerless, symbolizing the real-life dynamics that left her feeling unseen and undervalued. Upon waking, her anxiety mirrors the emotional toll of her past relationship, where her self-worth was often tied to Rob's unpredictable affirmations. Her description of the dream and the physical sensations upon waking—tight chest, heavy heart, and confusion—highlight how deeply emotional wounds can manifest in both the mind and body.

The hangover and paranoia after drinking illustrate how old habits can reignite familiar, unhealthy patterns. Alcohol temporarily lowers her guard, leading to overthinking and self-doubt. This mirrors her past reliance on Rob's inconsistent attention to stabilize her emotions, showing how external substances or people can become crutches during times of emotional instability.

Despite these struggles, Kellie demonstrates remarkable self-awareness. She recognizes how her past relationship and drinking habits negatively impacted her mental well-being, tying them to feelings of dependency and insecurity. Her ability to critically assess her thoughts and actions, even while feeling anxious and unbalanced, is a testament to her emotional growth. For example, she takes active steps to regain control by checking her phone for potential regrettable actions, rejecting a new contact from a bar, and reaffirming her resolve to avoid engaging in behaviors that might derail her progress.

Kellie's reflections reveal her resilience. She acknowledges emotional turbulence but resolves to maintain her commitment to sobriety and self-care. By examining her reactions and reaffirming her boundaries, she actively resists falling back into old patterns. Her quiet demeanor at breakfast suggests a moment of introspection rather than withdrawal, as she processes her emotions and recommits her healing journey.

Kellie recognizes that her choice to remain silent and avoid reaching out to Rob has created space for healing and self-awareness.

Silence, in this context, is not a void but a means of rebuilding her emotional foundation. By identifying alcohol as a trigger for her anxiety and negative thought patterns, she gains clarity on what behaviors to avoid in the future. Despite moments of vulnerability, she remains focused on her long-term goals—self-love, independence, and emotional stability.

Kellie's journal entry captures the complexity of emotional healing—marked by setbacks, breakthroughs, and the delicate balance of addressing past wounds while moving forward. Her willingness to confront difficult emotions head-on and her reflective mindset highlights considerable progress on her journey. This moment, though challenging, serves as a reminder of her strength and capacity for self-compassion, paving the way for continued growth and empowerment.

Journal Entry—Day 32: Mood—a combination of self-awareness, determination, and resolve, tempered by a lingering sense of frustration and regret over past choices.

The weekend getaway to Palm Desert was eye-opening—it resurfaced my wounded self and helped me understand where I stand in my relationship with Rob. I felt small, undervalued, and disempowered. The drive home was different. I felt a deep anger toward myself for allowing Rob to walk all over me. Why did I take the focus off myself?

I still wrestle with thoughts of self-blame, wondering if my weaknesses allowed Rob to treat me the way he did. Did he project my insecurities back at me? Is that why he never took me seriously? These questions pull me into a loop of negative self-talk. But then I remind myself: why should I blame myself when I had pure intentions? I cared for him deeply. My efforts to prioritize him—following his plans, making him the center of attention, were my way of showing love and compromise.

But Rob did not respect my time. He made me feel insecure because he never reassured me about where we stood. I was always on edge, fearing the relationship might end at any moment. Yet, these realizations no longer carry the weight they once did. What matters now is the choice to put myself first.

This healing journey so far has taught me to control my emotions and look deeply within. I've learned to set goals that work in my favor. I've also accepted that I can overanalyze Rob's actions all I want, but I can never control another person's behavior.

The only control I have is over my own choices and actions. For the next three months, I am dedicating myself to my physical, emotional, and mental well-being. I will reject excuses, silence negative self-talk, and commit to my transformation. I envision the best version of myself—confident, focused, committed, and consistent. The pounding headache from my brief relapse serves as a reminder to stay the course and not fall back into old habits and patterns.

Fear of change and uncertainty has held me back for too long. I see now that my resistance to discomfort has been my downfall, keeping me tethered to familiar but toxic patterns. It is time to push beyond that fear and reclaim myself. This journey is about discovering my authentic self, no longer doubting my worth, and finding happiness within—unshaped by others, circumstances, or fleeting events.

I refuse to return to patterns that no longer serve me. This transformation is for me, and I won't apologize for pursuing it. I will sit in silence, keep my goals to myself, and focus on actions over announcements. For the next three months, I will train like a warrior—rejecting vices, transforming, upgrading, and thriving. Everything I need is already within me.

I will become stronger, physically, and emotionally. I will re-emerge as someone who values herself, recognizes her worth, and no longer needs external validation. This journey is about breaking through old psychological barriers and changing the beliefs I hold about myself.

Silence has taught me to choose peace over drama and distance over disrespect. I've embraced the power of "going ghost," stepping back, and letting actions speak louder than words. Each success fuels my confidence. I no longer crave fleeting dopamine hits or temporary gratification. I have survived the breakup, maintained my silence, and proven my resilience. I know now that I can set meaningful goals and crush them. Taking back my power means no longer chasing—it means standing still, strong in my own worth.

For too long, I floated through life without intention, driven by habits rather than purpose. I realize now that the most irreplaceable asset I have is time. I won't waste it on people or things that don't align with my goals. This journey is about prioritizing my needs and unapologetically pursuing my dreams. It is about reclaiming my time, my focus, and my happiness—for me and no one else.

Reflection & Analysis: Reclaiming My Identity & Embracing Change

Kellie's journal entry begins with her acknowledgment of past wounds and the behaviors that perpetuated her pain. She openly confronts the reality of how her relationship with Rob left her feeling "small, undervalued, and disempowered." This self-awareness is crucial, as it signals a turning point in her healing process.

Kellie recognizes the ways she compromised herself to accommodate Rob, going along with his plans and prioritizing his needs over her own. Her analysis of Rob's lack of reassurance and respect for her time underscores her growing understanding of the imbalance in their dynamic. She identifies a recurring cycle of self-doubt, overthinking, and seeking validation from Rob, noting that it stunted her emotional growth and made her reliant on external affirmations. This realization is pivotal for breaking free from those patterns.

Kellie grapples with self-blame, questioning whether her insecurities enabled Rob to undervalue her. Yet, she also defends her intentions, acknowledging that her care for him was genuine. This internal conflict highlights a common struggle in healing: reconciling past actions and intentions with the pain caused by the relationship. Kellie wonders if Rob's behavior was a projection of her insecurities, leading her to further self-blame. However, she wisely concludes that she cannot control someone else's behavior and shifts her focus to her own growth. By reframing her narrative, Kellie moves from self-blame to self-empowerment, deciding to prioritize her needs and stop making excuses for toxic patterns.

Kellie's resolve to dedicate the next three months to her physical, emotional, and mental well-being marks a shift in her mindset. She transitions from dwelling in the past to envisioning a future where she is confident, focused, and committed to her own happiness. Her decision to "choose peace over drama" and "distance over disrespect" reflects a newfound maturity and self-respect. Kellie's silence is not avoidance; it is a deliberate strategy to focus inward and build her strength. By setting tangible goals and envisioning her "best self," Kellie creates a roadmap for her journey. She acknowledges that this transformation will require discipline and a willingness to confront discomfort, but her determination to "train like a warrior" signifies her readiness for the challenge.

Kellie identifies fear of change and uncertainty as barriers that kept her in familiar yet toxic patterns. Her decision to push through this fear marks a significant psychological breakthrough. She recognizes that her old habits didn't align with her authentic self and vows to reclaim her identity. This realization is empowering, as it shifts her focus from external validation to internal fulfillment. Kellie's declaration that she is "doing this for me" highlights her desire to take ownership of her life. She no longer wants to be defined by relationships or circumstances but instead seeks to cultivate her happiness from within.

Kellie ends her entry with a bold affirmation of her intentions. Her confidence in her ability to transform and thrive is evident in her commitment to consistency, self-respect, and prioritizing her time. She acknowledges that time is an irreplaceable asset and resolves to use it wisely, focusing on people and activities that align with her goals and values. By taking actionable steps toward her goals, Kellie realizes she can rebuild her confidence and self-esteem. Her belief in incremental progress underscores her resilience and optimism.

Kellie's journal entry is both a reflection of her past struggles and a manifesto for her future growth. It captures the complexity of healing—navigating self-blame, mourning lost time, and battling insecurities—while also celebrating the strength and clarity she has gained.

Her journey is a testament to the power of self-awareness, intentionality, and perseverance. This entry reflects a woman who is no longer willing to be defined by her past but instead seeks to reclaim her power, embrace change, and create a life of purpose and self-respect. Her determination to "go all in" on herself is inspiring and serves as a reminder that transformation begins with a choice to prioritize one's own well-being.

Journal Entry—Day 33: Mood—optimistic, empowered, and resolute.

I woke up feeling renewed and refreshed. The headache is gone, and after a restful sleep, I feel ready to embrace the day. I am determined to attend my yoga sculpt class after work and stop by Whole Foods to restock on oat milk, honey, and tea. I am looking forward to making a nourishing dinner tonight and taking Bailey out for a long walk under the evening sky. Most importantly, I need to reserve my flight to Texas for Debi and David's wedding.

Today, I want to hold onto this sense of optimism and happiness. I have come to understand that happiness doesn't fall from the sky, it's something we actively create. Life feels like a battlefield at times, and that is why I have embraced journaling, especially during the post-breakup months. Writing down my thoughts and tentative plans for the day has become a ritual that helps me process my emotions and untangle my feelings.

Although confronting my thoughts can be grueling, this habit has brought me clarity and a sense of purpose. Journaling in the morning sets the tone for my day, while my evening reflections help me find closure and understanding. It is practice that has taught me to face my emotions with courage and transform them into goals. Waking up now feels different—I approach each day with a conqueror's mindset.

Choosing myself and striving for excellence over mediocrity is my priority. It means rising early, hitting the yoga studio, honing my skills, and facing obstacles head-on. Over the past month, I have stepped out of my comfort zone and embraced the grind. The healing process has taught me that happiness is not handed to you—it's achieved. Small wins each day bring me balance, joy, and a sense of progress.

This silence I have embraced has become my teacher. It helps me cut out distractions and focus on what truly matters. It teaches me gratitude—to wake up and see each day as an opportunity to heal, to feel, to experience, and to love myself. There is something deeply empowering about realizing I can shape my destiny through daily choices.

I am learning that happiness isn't found—it's built. With every small victory, I am constructing a life that feels fulfilling and true to who I am. And for that, I am deeply grateful.

Reflection & Analysis: Rising with Purpose

Kellie begins her day with a renewed sense of purpose and energy, appreciating the progress she has made in her healing journey. Her reflections demonstrate a deliberate focus on self-improvement, gratitude, and the active pursuit of happiness.

There is a tone of determination as she outlines her plans and reaffirms her commitment to building a better version of herself. Kellie's journal entry reflects a pivotal moment in her healing journey marked by a sense of control, gratitude, and empowerment. Her tone conveys a shift from reactive to proactive living, showcasing her determination to rebuild her life on her own terms. Through this reflection, she highlights the importance of small, intentional steps toward growth and self-improvement.

Kellie's decision to take ownership of her happiness represents a critical breakthrough. She acknowledges that happiness is not a passive occurrence but an intentional effort. By focusing on habits like journaling, goal setting, and self-care, she demonstrates her resolve to reclaim her life and move away from the dependency and insecurity that may have defined her past relationships.

Journaling serves as a therapeutic tool for Kellie, enabling her to process her emotions and set clear intentions for the day. This practice underscores her growing emotional intelligence, as she confronts complex feelings and transforms them into actionable goals. It also highlights the value of mindfulness in her journey to personal clarity.

Kellie's focus on daily victories, such as attending yoga, preparing a nourishing meal, or simply finding gratitude, highlights the incremental nature of growth. These small achievements create a cumulative sense of progress and balance, emphasizing the importance of consistency and effort in building a fulfilling life. She views silence not as emptiness but as a space for introspection and self-awareness. By cutting out distractions, Kellie can recalibrate her priorities and focus on cultivating a deeper relationship with herself. This silence becomes a metaphor for her journey inward, where she discovers her capacity for resilience and self-love.

Kellie's expression of gratitude for the opportunity to create her destiny reflects a fundamental change in perspective. Instead of lamenting her circumstances, she chooses to see them as a foundation for growth. This optimism signals a deeper acceptance of her past and a readiness to embrace the future.

Kellie's entry demonstrates a profound transformation in her mindset. She has moved from being reactive—seeking validation from external sources like a past relationship—to pro-active, taking deliberate steps to nurture her well-being. Her acknowledgment that happiness is built rather than found indicates an internalization of key lessons learned through her struggles. By embracing the grind of self-improvement and rejecting mediocrity, she signals her readiness to evolve into a stronger, more confident version of herself.

This reflection serves as an inspiring reminder that healing is a process of both discovery and creation. Kellie's journey exemplifies how setbacks can be transformed into steppingstones, and how intentional action can lead to profound personal breakthroughs.

Journal Entry—Day 34: Mood—joyful, confident, and accomplished.

Booked my roundtrip flight to Dallas-Fort Worth, Texas—check! Now, the next task: finding the perfect dress for my friend Debi's wedding. Debi, the bride, had requested that her seven close friends from California wear colorful dresses paired with cowgirl boots for the photoshoot, a playful nod to the Texas vibe. The idea of shopping for a new outfit is always exciting, but finding the right dress? That is where the real adventure begins.

I spent the day browsing a few shops and boutiques on Fashion Island, determined to find something both stylish and flattering. Then, a dress caught my eye: a strapless, mesh, midi-length bodycon in a deep floral burgundy. It was stunning, but I hesitated—would it fit well? I grabbed a medium, tried it on, and to my surprise, it was loose. Could I be a size small? Skeptically, I asked for a smaller size. When I slipped it on, it fit like a glove. The silhouette hugged me in all the right places, and the confidence that comes with a perfectly fitting dress is simply unmatched. That moment felt like magic—I had found the dress.

Next stop: Boot Barn. I was on the hunt for cowgirl boots to complete the outfit and, oh, did I find a gem. A pair of beige-brown boots with intricate stitching that radiated personality and charm caught my attention. They had the perfect blend of classic Western style with a modern twist. Sliding them on, I knew they were the ones. My first pair of cowgirl boots, and they couldn't be more perfect.

Mission accomplished. The dress, the boots—it all came together seamlessly. I left feeling thrilled and confident, ready to celebrate Debi's special day in an outfit that feels both authentic and fabulous. What more could a girl ask for?

Reflection & Analysis: Perfect Fit—Embracing Joy, Style, and Self-Love

Kellie expresses excitement and enthusiasm throughout her shopping experience, from the initial thrill of finding a beautiful dress to the satisfaction of discovering it fits perfectly. Her mood lifts even further as she finds the ideal pair of cowgirl boots, completing her outfit with a sense of pride and happiness. Overall, Kellie exudes a vibrant positivity, fueled by her success in preparing for her friend's wedding and the confidence that comes with looking and feeling her best.

Kellie's journal entry reflects a moment of lighthearted joy and confidence that comes from personal accomplishment and self-expression. The narrative captures her excitement and satisfaction in finding the perfect outfit for her friend's wedding, symbolizing more than just a shopping trip, it signifies self-discovery, growth, and reclaiming her confidence.

The moment she realizes a smaller dress size fits her perfectly highlights her growing confidence in her physical transformation and self-perception. This is a subtle understanding of the hard work and discipline she has put into her personal growth journey. The joy and pride she experiences are not just about aesthetics but also a deeper validation of her efforts to heal and transform.

Kellie's happiness is rooted in achieving small, tangible victories, finding the perfect dress and boots. These moments remind her of the satisfaction that comes from tackling challenges, no matter how trivial they may seem. It shows her ability to find happiness in day-to-day accomplishments, reinforcing the importance of celebrating progress in her healing process.

The tone of this entry is notably lighter than previous reflections. It signals that Kellie is allowing herself to embrace joy and optimism without the overshadowing weight of past emotional turmoil. She is starting to prioritize fun and indulge in activities that make her feel good about herself, highlighting a healthier balance in her life.

The chosen outfit—floral dress, and cowgirl boots—represents Kellie's readiness to embrace new experiences and show up for her friends with confidence. The boots carry a cultural charm and a touch of novelty, symbolizing her desire to try something new and step out of her comfort zone. The entry shows how Kellie is making choices that reflect self-care and self-love. Her excitement over fitting into a smaller dress size and finding the perfect boots underscores her journey toward rediscovering herself.

Kellie is reconnecting with a part of herself that can find delight in small moments, such as shopping and preparing for an event. This is a significant shift from her earlier entries, which were more introspective and heavier with emotional processing.

This entry suggests Kellie is gaining momentum in her healing journey. She's finding ways to enjoy life while building confidence, indicating progress in moving forward from her past struggles. Kellie's journal entry showcases a moment of vibrancy and joy, offering a snapshot of her personal transformation and the strength she's rediscovering in herself.

Journal Entry—Day 35: Mood—hopeful, reflective, and anticipatory.

After a 3.5-hour flight, I arrived in Fort Worth, Dallas, Texas, under the warm September night breeze. It was a sultry evening, nearly scorching at 97 degrees. The sprawling freeways and flat, expansive terrain of Texas immediately offered a stark contrast to the familiarity of home. As I took in this new city, I felt a refreshing shift in perspective. The vast openness of Texas mirrored the endless possibilities life holds, reminding me that what often seems overwhelming in the moment may not be as insurmountable as it appears when viewed from a broader lens.

The Uber ride to the hotel gave me time to reflect, soaking in the sights of this unfamiliar environment. Upon arriving at the hotel, I was greeted by the familiar faces of friends also staying there. The excitement was palpable, as everyone eagerly anticipated the big wedding tomorrow.

As I retreated to my hotel room, the change in ambiance filled me with a quiet sense of renewal. The unfamiliar setting brought a glimmer of hope and anticipation, a subtle reminder of the beauty in exploring the unknown. Tonight, I will take the time to rest and recharge, preparing myself for tomorrow's celebration of love and friendship, a special day for Debi and a memorable experience for all of us.

Reflection & Analysis: Wide Open Spaces—Embracing New Horizons

Kellie highlights the transformative effect of an unfamiliar environment. The wide Texas landscapes and the unfamiliar cityscape inspire her to reevaluate her current challenges. This suggests that stepping out of her routine helps her see problems as less overwhelming and opens her mind to new possibilities. Her description of Texas emphasizes vastness and openness, which metaphorically aligns with her thoughts on the expansiveness of opportunities in life. This moment of clarity indicates a deepening of self-awareness and emotional resilience.

Kellie's mood reflects hopefulness and a budding optimism. Her ability to derive inspiration from her surroundings shows emotional maturity and a willingness to embrace change. By recognizing that what once seemed insurmountable is manageable with perspective, she is building a healthier mindset and demonstrating personal growth.

The upcoming wedding and the chance to reconnect with friends add a layer of excitement and joy to the entry. This shows Kellie's appreciation for social bonds and her ability to find happiness in shared experiences. At the same time, her retreat to the hotel room and reflection signals a balance between social connection and the need for solitude to process her thoughts.

The entry uses vivid imagery to convey both physical and emotional landscapes, from the warm Texas breeze to the vast freeways. It demonstrates Kellie's shift in perspective and emotional state. The tone is reflective yet forward-looking, with a subtle blend of gratitude for the present and hope for the future.

This journal entry highlights Kellie's growing ability to find positivity and meaning in new experiences. It also shows her progress in managing her emotions and reframing challenges as opportunities for growth. Her willingness to embrace a change of scenery and its accompanying lessons speaks to her evolving self-reliance and optimism.

Kellie's journal entry marks another step in Kellie's journey toward emotional resilience, self-discovery, and a renewed sense of hope for the future. She expresses hope and a renewed perspective as she observes the vastness of Texas and its symbolism for possibilities and new beginnings. Her tone is reflective, as she contemplates how stepping out of her usual environment helps her reframe her problems and see them in a less daunting light. There is also an undertone of excitement and anticipation for her friend's wedding and the shared joy of reconnecting with friends in a celebratory setting.

Journal Entry—Day 36: Mood—empowered, reflective, and indifferent.

The wedding venue at Lucky Spur Ranch was breathtaking—an elegant blend of rustic southern charm. The outdoor ceremony, set against a backdrop of flowing creeks and sprawling trees, was nothing short of magical. As Debi walked down the aisle, radiant in her bridal glow, she met her handsome groom, David. Tears welled in my eyes as I listened to their heartfelt vows.

Debi's words moved me deeply: she shared how David had always made her feel special and beautiful, even on her tough days, when she doubted herself. She spoke of how his unwavering acceptance of her, flaws, and all, made her feel like the smartest and most beautiful woman in the world. And the way David looked at her said it all—his love was pure and absolute, a promise to cherish her and do whatever it takes to keep her happy.

In that moment, I felt a revelation wash over me—a realization of what true love looks like. It's unconditional, steady, and affirming. It does not make you question your worth or second-guess where you stand. It does not confuse or judge. It is simply a wholehearted acceptance and adoration of the person you deeply care about. Witnessing their love firsthand was both inspiring and healing, as if I was being reminded of the love I truly deserve.

After the ceremony, we transitioned into the reception barn, where an evening of dinner and dancing awaited. It was a dazzling celebration of Debi and David's union. I dined, danced, and laughed freely, savoring the joy of the moment. I even met Ryan, a native Texan, who quickly became my dance partner for the night. Ryan's openness and charm stood out. He was conscientious and thoughtful, always checking in to see if I needed water or a break from dancing and patiently waiting by my side until I was ready to hit the dance floor again. His kind and attentive nature made the evening even more memorable.

Amidst the fun and excitement, my phone buzzed with an unexpected text. It was Rob. Isn't it funny how a man seems to sense when you are genuinely enjoying life and moving on? His message was simple: "Just wanted to say hi."

Surprisingly, I felt little to no reaction. There was no rush of emotions, no rekindled longing—just indifference. I was so immersed in the moment that the notification barely registered. Still, I took a selfie with Ryan and sent it to Rob, replying, "I'm at a friend's wedding in Texas." Rob responded with amazement at the timing, complimenting my dress and hair. He made no mention of Ryan, but it was clear he knew how to time his texts perfectly.

Yet, for the first time, I didn't care. I left my phone in my purse and returned to the dance floor, where life was happening. The emotional attachment I once felt to Rob seemed to have dissolved. That night, I was truly living in the moment—dancing, laughing, and enjoying myself without the weight of past entanglements. Rob's text, once something I might have clung to, had no power over me anymore. And that realization felt liberating!

Reflection & Analysis: Dancing In My Own Light

Kellie begins the entry feeling uplifted and inspired by the wedding, witnessing true love and connection between Debi and David, which prompts her to reflect on what she deserves in a relationship. As the night progresses, Kellie experiences a sense of freedom and detachment when she receives a text from Rob, no longer feeling emotional attachment or concern about his message. Instead, she is fully engaged in enjoying the moment, dancing, and having fun without being weighed down by past emotional entanglements. Her mood shows signs of personal growth, embracing her own happiness and moving forward without being affected by Rob's presence in her life.

Kellie's journal entry reveals a significant shift in her emotional and mental state, showing her movement toward personal growth and emotional independence. The entry starts with Kellie observing and reflecting on the wedding between Debi and David. The sincerity of their vows and the unconditional love they express toward each other make Kellie think deeply about the nature of true love. She describes love as something that "doesn't make you second guess or question your worth," something she has longed for but has not yet experienced in her own relationships. This reflection indicates Kellie's evolving understanding of what she deserves in love, one that is mutual, unconditional, and free of confusion. It is a realization that not only highlights the emotional maturity she has developed since her breakup but also signals her growing awareness that she should no longer accept relationships that make her feel insecure or uncertain.

The tone of the entry shifts as Kellie becomes more centered on herself, enjoying the celebration without feeling the need for validation from others. She embraces the fun of the night, dancing and enjoying herself without the weight of her past relationship with Rob. Her interaction with Ryan, the new acquaintance, is a key moment in the entry. Although she enjoys his company and the attention he gives her, there is no indication that she is emotionally invested in him or seeking validation through him. Her focus remains on her own enjoyment and the present moment, suggesting that she is learning to cultivate her own happiness, independent of external sources.

The most profound moment of the entry comes when Kellie receives a text from Rob. In the past, such a message may have sent her spiraling into doubt, longing, or uncertainty. However, this time, she reacts with indifference—she does not feel the emotional weight she once did when hearing from him. Kellie's lack of emotional reaction signifies a shift in her mindset. It shows that she is no longer seeking reassurance from Rob and can separate herself emotionally from the past relationship. By sending Rob a selfie without expecting anything more, Kellie demonstrates a level of detachment that is a significant breakthrough in her emotional healing process.

As the night continues, Kellie chooses to live in the moment, enjoying the celebration, dancing, and interacting with others without worrying about Rob's text or past emotional entanglements. This decision to leave her phone in her purse and stay fully immersed in the present suggests that Kellie is finally gaining emotional freedom from her past relationships and, more importantly, from the anxieties and insecurities that accompanied them. Her ability to disengage from Rob and his influence marks a key turning point in her healing journeys, she is no longer fixated on the past or waiting for validation. Instead, she is embracing the joy of the present, and this shift represents the embodiment of self-empowerment and growth.

Kellie's reflection on the wedding vows is an indication of her growing emotional maturity and understanding of healthy, unconditional love. Her ability to enjoy the night, despite Rob's text, shows her personal growth and emotional independence. She no longer relies on Rob or anyone else for validation. Her indifferent response to Rob's message marks a significant emotional breakthrough, Kellie has finally separated herself from the past, allowing her to move forward with her life.

Kellie's focus on the present moment—free from the emotional baggage of the past—signals her progress in healing and self-discovery. She is fully embracing the joy and freedom of the present, which is a positive shift toward a more fulfilling and self-directed life. Overall, Kellie's mood can be described as empowered, free, and detached, reflecting a newfound strength in her ability to heal, prioritize herself, and live authentically. She begins the entry feeling uplifted and inspired by the wedding, witnessing true love and connection between Debi and David, which prompts her to reflect on what she deserves in a relationship.

As the night progresses, Kellie experiences a sense of freedom and detachment when she receives a text from Rob, no longer feeling emotional attachment or concern about his message. Instead, she is fully engaged in enjoying the moment, dancing, and having fun without being weighed down by past emotional entanglements. Her mood shows signs of personal growth, embracing her own happiness and moving forward without being affected by Rob's presence in her life.

Journal Entry—Day 37: Mood—reflective and empowered, with a mix of detachment and self-awareness.

Reflecting on last night at the wedding, it all felt surreal—a brief escape from the heavy cocoon of my past heartbreak. I allowed myself to have fun, to laugh, to dance without the constant weight of Rob looming over every moment. It was liberating, like finally breaking free from the endless loop of what-ifs that once defined our connection. And then, as if on cue, a text arrived from Rob—the very message I used to crave.

In that instant, a wave of clarity washed over me: I no longer felt the electric surge of longing that once tethered my heart to his. As my plane touched down in California, I couldn't help but notice how distant Rob had become, fading like a memory that no longer holds any power.

Once I disabled airplane mode, three new texts blinked on my screen. Rob was updating me about his life—a casual note about recovering from a virus he'd caught in Thailand, as if nothing had changed. His tone was indifferent, an echo of normalcy that no longer stirred my emotions. I asked, half-curious, what brought him to Thailand. His answer was as nonchalant as his texts—just a spontaneous trip, nothing more.

After a long, exhausting flight, I simply replied that I'd just landed and needed to move on with my day. Yet Rob persisted, shifting to small talk about the Packers—his favorite football team. At that moment, I realized I no longer cared. His excitement over the game fell flat, disconnected from the reality I had embraced. I curtly replied, "You must be stoked," and let the conversation fade.

Now, I sit with a quiet detachment, reflecting on what these messages mean—or rather, what they no longer mean to me. Was he testing the waters? Was it a fleeting whim or an attempt to throw crumbs my way? The truth is, I no longer feel the pull to reconnect. I've worked hard to break the cycle, and I'm not about to let myself fall back into that pattern.

In retrospect, this interaction marks a turning point in my healing. For so long, I believed closure had to come from Rob—a sign or a word to validate my pain. But now, I understand that real closure comes from within. His texts no longer hold sway over my heart. I have my own path and priorities, and for the first time, I'm walking away without looking back.

Reflection & Analysis: Detaching to Empower

Kellie reflects on her emotional journey, noting the stark difference between her past emotional reactions to Rob and her current, more composed state. She feels empowered by her ability to maintain boundaries and avoid being drawn back into a potentially unhealthy cycle. Although there is some lingering uncertainty about Rob's intentions, her detachment and focus on her own growth signify significant progress in her healing process.

Kellie's journal entry reflects a pivotal moment in her emotional journey, highlighting themes of growth, detachment, and caution. Kellie acknowledges a profound change in her emotional state regarding Rob. The longing and emotional upheaval she previously associated with him has faded, replaced by detachment and an objective perspective. This demonstrates her progress in moving past heartbreak. She recognizes her own reactions and behavior, noting her surprise at how cold and detached she came across in their recent interaction. This level of self-awareness is a testament to her growing emotional maturity.

Despite Rob's attempts to reconnect, Kellie remains wary of falling back into old patterns. Her cautious response indicates her commitment to prioritizing her emotional well-being and avoiding cycles that once caused her pain. Kellie's detachment from Rob's messages suggests that she is reclaiming her independence. Her focus shifts toward her own needs and life, rather than being preoccupied with his actions or intentions.

The entry shows how far Kellie has gone in her healing process. The emotional detachment she describes is not just about indifference to Rob but a deeper realization of her own value and priorities. While Kellie has made considerable progress, her uncertainty about

Rob's intentions reveals that some emotional ties or questions remain. However, her decision to disengage from the conversation suggests *strength and resolve*.

By acknowledging her coldness and deciding to uphold boundaries, Kellie demonstrates empowerment. She is actively choosing not to reenter a dynamic that could undermine her progress. Kellie is mindful of the cyclical nature of her past relationship with Rob and is taking conscious steps to break away from it. This awareness is crucial for her continued growth and emotional resilience. The entry reflects Kellie's shift from external validation (seeking connections or explanations from Rob) to internal validation (prioritizing her needs and well-being). Her newfound emotional distance from Rob's attempts to reconnect is a clear indicator of this change.

Kellie's journal entry captures a significant milestone in her healing process. She is no longer defined by her past relationship or consumed by Rob's actions. Her reflection on the interaction shows emotional maturity, self-awareness, and a determination to move forward with caution and confidence. This moment marks her reclaiming control over her emotional landscape and affirming her commitment to personal growth.

Part 2: Anatomy of No Contact

Reclaiming Your Inner Power

Journal Entry—Day 38:
Mood—contemplative and conflicted, with an undertone of cautious resolve.

Rob reached out—now what? I find myself in a quiet tug-of-war between the impulse to reconnect and the resolve to let go. Today, I pause to reflect on his sudden reappearance and, more importantly, on my own measured reaction—or, more accurately, my deliberate indifference. It's baffling to realize that while I've been healing, a part of me was still chasing the ghost of the love I thought I'd lost, driven by a need to prove myself, to show him a better version of me that might make him regret leaving.

Yet, as I sit in the silence I've chosen, I've discovered something invaluable: the ability to truly listen to my inner voice. That quiet space has allowed me to step back, examine my feelings, and reassess my choices before acting on raw emotion. In the past, I sought external validation to soothe my insecurities; now, I see how that endless search only drowned out the voice that champions my well-being and reminds me of my worth.

By choosing silence, I've reconnected with that inner strength—a clarity that guides me back to my core values. As I weigh Rob's intentions, I'm also forced to evaluate my own: What do I hope to gain by reopening a door that has long since closed? I remind myself of the progress I've made and the life I'm building—one that truly aligns with what I deserve.

I know my patterns too well. I've been swept away by emotion, lost in choices that left me frustrated, insecure, and paralyzed by the fear of loss. I will not fall into that trap again. Rob chose to leave, and in doing so, I already lost him. Now, it's time to honor my healing, to let my past insecurities fuel my ongoing growth.

I must ask myself: What void am I trying to fill? I refuse to conform to the old patterns that once held me captive. Instead, I choose transformation—to continue growing into the person I'm meant to be, someone who values herself enough to pursue what is truly fulfilling and healthy. I deserve better, and I am determined never to lose sight of that truth.

Reflection & Analysis: Quiet Tug-of-War: Reclaiming Self-Worth After Heartbreak

This journal entry is a powerful exploration of emotional growth and self-empowerment in the wake of a painful breakup. It captures the internal struggle Kellie faces when confronted with the possibility of reconnecting with someone who once held a significant part of her identity. Kellie describes an internal conflict—a battle between the lingering impulse to reach out to Rob and her newfound resolve to let go. The phrase "quiet tug-of-war" suggests that this is a deeply personal, almost silent struggle, one that contrasts with the dramatic, often overwhelming nature of heartbreak. This balance, or tension, is central to her journey of healing, as it highlights the shift from reacting impulsively to making deliberate, thoughtful choices.

Kellie has moved toward "deliberate indifference." Instead of falling back into old patterns of chasing external validation, she chooses to embrace silence as a way to listen to her inner voice. This is a significant milestone—it demonstrates that she is no longer willing to let her self-worth be dictated by Rob's actions or words. Her indifference is not apathy; it's a conscious decision that reflects her growing strength and self-respect.

Kellie is learning to tune in to her own needs, to reflect on her past actions, and to recognize the patterns that have held her captive. By re-engaging with her inner strength, she is able to challenge the old habits of seeking external affirmation. The clarity she finds in that silence allows her to realign with her core values and reassess her relationship with Rob—and with herself.

Kellie's reflection shows a deep self-awareness. She admits that she once chased a love that was, in reality, an illusion—a desperate attempt to prove her worth and win him back. This recognition of past behavior is critical for her transformation. It underscores the idea that healing often requires confronting uncomfortable truths about one's own vulnerabilities and learning from them.

Ultimately, the passage is a declaration of Kellie's commitment to self-growth. She questions what she truly hopes to gain by reopening the door to a relationship that has already shown its flaws. Instead, she reaffirms her determination to focus on building a life that aligns with her intrinsic values and worth. This shift—from dependency to self-reliance—is portrayed as both liberating and necessary for her continued emotional healing.

Journal Entry—Day 39: Mood—reflective, resolute, and empowered.

I am committing to staying on course and breaking free from the emotional swings and pull of wanting Rob. I now take full responsibility for my well-being and future. Only by looking at myself in the mirror and owning my destiny can I truly succeed. Healing is my responsibility, and I must see the situation for what it truly is.

Rob was never my partner in the way I needed. His priorities were elsewhere, and he was *disinterested* in building a genuine relationship with me. I must hear that *truth* loud and clear. The attention he gave me was minimal crumbs, at best. That is why I was never included in his life or activities. He controlled who he let in and kept me at arm's length. It's heartbreaking, but it's reality.

I cannot believe I wrestled with this issue for so long, subjecting myself to chaos. But now, I am choosing strength and boundaries.

I am disengaging because I refuse to be emotionally mistreated any longer. If a future relationship walks into my life, I know what I want: a partnership built on mutual respect, unity, and compromise. I want a bond where both people are emotionally and mentally strong, working together as one.

Rob was never ready for me. If he were, or if he is someday, he would *make it clear* by his words and actions that he wants me in his life. But he did not. Instead, our relationship was filled with fear—my fear of facing the truth and of rejection. That fear left me in emotional distress because Rob never provided the security or reassurance I needed.

Taking time in silence has been painful but necessary. It has given me the space to process and grow, to sacrifice chaos for the greater outcome of emotional maturity. Real love, whether for myself or with someone else—requires a different level of emotional and mental readiness.

When I reflect on my time with Rob, I see it now for what it was. I felt confused, distressed, anxious, insecure, doubtful, jealous, co-dependent, and stuck in a cycle of unfulfilled promises and psychological chaos. The relationship lacked progress, clarity, and the unconditional love I deserved. Rob offered only a conditional affection—texts and small gestures that kept me at bay but never close enough. No wonder I felt so insecure.

I now forgive myself for staying in that chaotic relationship. I also forgive Rob—not for him, but for me. Forgiveness is my path to peace, and I am choosing it for myself.

Reflection & Analysis: Blueprint for Renewal

Kellie demonstrates a deep introspection about her past relationship with Rob and a clear determination to move forward. While there are moments of sadness and heartbreak as she acknowledges the reality of her past, her tone also conveys strength, self-awareness, and a commitment to personal growth and healing. Her mood reflects a transition from pain and uncertainty to clarity and empowerment.

Kellie's journal entry represents a pivotal moment of self-reflection, growth, and empowerment. It captures her transition from emotional turmoil to a place of clarity and determination. The entry is a testament to her inner strength and her willingness to confront the hard truths about her relationship with Rob. Kellie has come to terms with the fact that she was not Rob's priority. She explicitly identifies the lack of reciprocity and emotional security in their relationship. This acknowledgment is significant because it shows her ability to move beyond denial and idealization, seeing the relationship for what it truly was.

Kellie emphasizes taking personal responsibility for her well-being and future, demonstrating a pro-active mindset. She recognizes that healing is her responsibility, not something dependent on Rob or external circumstances. This self-awareness marks a shift from dependency to autonomy. She outlines the emotional chaos she experienced in the relationship: *insecurity, doubt, and lack of inclusion* in Rob's life. By detailing these patterns, she shows her ability to analyze the relationship critically, which is essential for avoiding similar dynamics in the future. Kellie's decision to disengage and build strength and boundaries is a powerful affirmation of her commitment to self-respect. She refuses to tolerate emotional neglect or manipulation, demonstrating her resolve to *prioritize her emotional health*.

Kellie forgives herself for staying in the relationship despite its flaws, which is a crucial step in releasing guilt and shame. Her forgiveness for Rob, not for his sake but for her own peace, signifies emotional maturity and a desire to free herself from lingering resentment. Kellie articulates her desire for a partnership based on unity, emotional maturity, and mutual respect. This forward-looking perspective reflects her growth and her commitment to seeking a relationship that aligns with her values and needs.

While there is lingering sadness, Kellie's tone is one of empowerment and resolution. Her ability to analyze the past while focusing on personal growth underscores her emotional transformation and resilience. Kellie's journal entry is a powerful narrative of self-discovery and empowerment. It highlights her journey from emotional dependence and chaos to a place of clarity, strength, and forgiveness. By recognizing unhealthy dynamics and committing to personal growth, she paves the way for a healthier, more fulfilling future. This entry is not just a reflection of the past but a blueprint for the person she is becoming.

Journal Entry Day 40: Mood~Reflective, Resolute, and More Empowered.

I realize now that what kept me stuck were endless cycles of stress and emotional turmoil—an incessant spiral fueled by trauma bonds, deep-seated insecurities, and a haunting sense of abandonment that left me feeling unworthy. The roots of my self-doubt lie in unresolved loneliness, old wounds from childhood, and societal pressures that have clashed with who I truly am. Failed relationships only deepened this toxic cycle, and for too long, I struggled to break free.

Today, I choose reality. I accept things as they are, and in that raw acceptance, I ask: what comes next? In the profound silence that surrounds me, I find a guide—a space that allows me to prioritize my well-being and face the truth head-on. Healing is uncomfortable, even painful, but I now understand that growth demands I lean into the discomfort rather than run from it.

I'm letting go of the need to control every outcome or to wish things were different. In this silence, I have discovered the strength to sit with my pain, to confront it honestly, and to trust that I cannot control others, only my own intentions. This clarity empowers me to break free from the cycles that once held me captive.

My body, my heart, and my very soul resonate with this truth. When love goes unreturned, my nerves scream with anxiety, yet I have endured that suffering. With every battle fought, I am emerging a little stronger—learning to show up for myself, breaking the chains of toxic attachment, and rejecting the crumbs of attention I once craved.

I choose freedom—a life where peace triumphs over perpetual turmoil. I imagine what it would be like to feel secure in love, a love that isn't a game or a constant chase for validation. I know I am worthy of a relationship built on genuine care, trust, and mutual respect. I deserve to be someone's priority, not an afterthought.

The road to confidence is long and challenging, but I am committed to loving and prioritizing myself. I know now that I am worthy of love, commitment, and respect—and I will no longer settle for anything less.

Reflection & Analysis: Breaking the Cycle: Embracing Reality and Reclaiming My Worth

Kellie's journal entry is a deeply personal declaration of liberation and self-awareness. It begins with Kellie pinpointing the sources of her emotional stagnation—the ceaseless cycle of stress, trauma bonds, and deep-rooted insecurities. She traces her self-doubt to unresolved loneliness, childhood wounds, and societal pressures, which have all conspired to keep her trapped in a toxic loop of failed relationships and self-abandonment.

What stands out is the transformation in her mindset. Kellie contrasts her past state of being ensnared in these destructive patterns with her current decision to "choose reality." In embracing the truth of her situation, she rejects the need to control external outcomes and instead turns inward. The silence around her becomes not a void, but a space for reflection and healing—an invitation to sit with her pain, understand it, and ultimately grow from it.

Her language conveys a palpable sense of empowerment. As she acknowledges that she cannot control others but can direct her own intentions, she reclaims the power that was once held hostage by her toxic attachments. The passage is raw and unflinching in its portrayal of the physical and emotional toll of unreciprocated love, yet it also offers hope: Kellie recognizes that enduring suffering has made her stronger and more resilient.

Ultimately, Kellie's journey is framed as a path toward freedom—a freedom defined not by the absence of pain, but by the ability to prioritize her well-being and self-worth above all else. She envisions a future where love is not a relentless pursuit for validation, but a secure, mutually respectful bond. The commitment to self-love and the determination to stop settling for less than she deserves are powerful indicators of her progress and emerging confidence.

In essence, this passage captures a pivotal moment of awakening: the realization that true healing comes from within, and that by facing her discomfort head-on, she can break free from old patterns and rebuild her life on her own terms.

Journal Entry Day 41: Mood~A Combination of Determination, Empowerment, and Self-Awareness.

A matter of fact is that the truth will set you free. Not accepting the truth is like living in blissful ignorance—like lying to yourself to avoid confronting reality or controlling the outcome. The truth is that Rob led me on. Yes, the truth can set you free, but first, it will make you angry.

I have learned that if I want to be happy with where I am today, I must change the habits and behaviors that kept me stuck in the past.

Change is hard. Change is uncomfortable. It felt strange when I started my fitness journey because it was new and unfamiliar. But today, I chose to celebrate my progress by acknowledging and honoring the steps I've already taken toward self-improvement.

I am no longer chained to a toxic relationship with Rob. No more waiting for text messages, obsessing over a relationship, or seeking his validation. I've broken free from those cycles. Instead of being cooped up on my phone, I've thrown myself into my fitness journey, embraced healthier eating habits, and stopped wasting time on things or people that don't deserve it.

I am unapologetically pursuing my goals and dreams. I've shifted my focus to putting myself first. Now, I get confidence hits instead of fleeting dopamine rushes. I stay focused and busy with my aspirations, replacing toxic relationships with personal development goals. I have traded alcohol for water, binge-watching for reading, and overthinking for action. Yoga and exercise routines have become my new therapy.

I have replaced fear with determination, and instead of chasing Rob's attention or validation, I am chasing my purpose. Consistency, discipline, and showing up for myself have become my anchor. I am making slow and steady progress—emotionally, physically, and mentally.

This is how I have displaced the old habits and routines that once brought me unhappiness, despair, and anxiety. It is about replacing the old with the new habits that are good for me. This is what throwing myself into the discomfort of pain looks and feels like. It is acknowledging the hurt while still showing up for myself. Collectively, these new habits have helped me not just survive but *thrive* through moments of emotional silence.

Reflection & Analysis: Embracing Change

Kellie is processing her emotional journey with a clear focus on personal growth and change. She recognizes the discomfort of growth but embraces it as necessary for her well-being. There is an underlying sense of pride in her progress, as well as a firm commitment to putting herself first and breaking free from the toxic patterns of her past relationship. While she acknowledges past pain, she is actively choosing to move forward, prioritizing her goals, and cultivating healthier habits. Overall, Kellie's mood seems strong, focused, and resolute.

Kellie's journal entry reveals deep self-reflection, emotional growth, and a commitment to change. She begins by confronting a difficult truth about her past relationship with Rob, acknowledging how it was built on deception and unreciprocated feelings. This acknowledgment marks a pivotal moment of self-liberation, even if the truth initially stirs up anger or frustration. Kellie seems to understand that healing requires confronting uncomfortable truths and being honest with herself.

A significant theme in the entry is the idea of "change." Kellie recognizes that to improve her emotional, physical, and mental well-being, she must shift her habits and behaviors. There is an understanding that change is challenging, but it's essential for her growth. Kellie contrasts her past behaviors, such as waiting for validation from Rob, with her new habits, like focusing on fitness, health, and personal goals. The language she uses reflects a shift from passivity to agency: "I am unapologetically going after my goals and dreams," and "I am putting myself first."

What stands out is her sense of empowerment. She describes replacing unhealthy habits—such as seeking validation and spending time on distractions—with healthier, self-affirming behaviors like exercising, eating better, reading, and focusing on personal growth. There is a distinct sense of "taking control" of her life and her future. Kellie's use of phrases like "confidence hits instead of dopamine hits" and "staying consistent" highlights her awareness of the value of self-discipline and long-term goals over short-term emotional gratification.

Kellie's acknowledgment of the discomfort that comes with change (described as "throwing myself in pain") is significant. It shows that she is not shying away from the difficult parts of healing—emotional pain and self-discipline—but is instead choosing to face them head-on. The concept of "pain" is reframed here as a vehicle for growth, rather than something to avoid. She demonstrates acceptance that healing, growth, and change are *not linear* and require ongoing effort and self-compassion.

Kellie's entry shows a remarkable shift in mindset. From feeling stuck and overwhelmed by her relationship with Rob, she has moved into a space where she prioritizes herself. She expresses pride in her progress, even if it is slow and steady, and is making conscious decisions to prioritize actions and habits that align with her long-term vision of well-being. Her reflections show self-awareness, emotional maturity, and a strong resolve to maintain her independence and self-worth. In essence, Kellie's journal entry is an expression of empowerment and self-responsibility. She is taking full ownership of her journey, recognizing that her happiness and well-being depend on her ability to change unhealthy patterns and focus on what truly serves her.

Journal Entry—Day 42: Mood—reflective and resolute, with undertones of lingering sadness and self-empowerment.

Letting go of someone you really care about is undeniably hard. I must constantly remind myself to choose myself and prioritize my well-being. This breakup has been a profound lesson—it is shown me that love doesn't simply disappear overnight, and unloving someone isn't immediate or effortless unless that love was never real to begin with. I find myself still holding onto the warmth of the good times, replaying the memories that once brought me joy.

Yet, as I navigate the process of moving on from Rob and our "situationship," I have realized there is another layer to confront—*disappointment* in myself. It is a bitter pill to swallow, acknowledging that no matter how deep our bond felt or how happy those memories were, life has a way of pushing us onto different paths. And I know I must move forward, no matter how difficult it feels.

I've learned to shift my perspective from "Why is this happening to me?" to "What is this teaching me?" Letting go means accepting what happened, honoring the lessons, and continuing to live with intention. Life is filled with crossroads, and though today may be difficult, I hold onto the belief that tomorrow will bring new opportunities, growth, and clarity.

The person I once loved the most has taught me a powerful truth: to love more wisely and to protect my heart. Despite all the self-disappointment I have faced, I'm choosing to love and honor myself. This journey has shown me that everything I need is already within me. I have come so far, and now I focus on building a life that fulfills and excites me—without relying on anyone else to define my happiness.

Reflection & Analysis: Healing Through Reflection

Kellie is reflective as she contemplates her emotions, the lessons from her breakup, and her personal growth. Her acknowledgment of the good memories and the pain of moving on shows her deep introspection. She is also resolute in her decision to prioritize herself and embrace a healthier, more self-sufficient life. Despite the challenges, she expresses determination to let go and focus on her own well-being. The mood carries an underlying sadness tied to the lingering affection and disappointment in herself, but it is balanced by a tone of hopefulness and self-love as she chooses to embrace the future with optimism.

Kellie's journal entry reveals a deep journey of emotional growth and self-awareness, underscoring the complexity of healing after a breakup. She openly admits that letting go is difficult and acknowledges her lingering attachment to Rob. This vulnerability is a crucial step in her healing process, as it demonstrates her willingness to confront her emotions rather than suppress them. Her shift from asking "why is this happening to me" to "what's this trying to teach me" signifies an evolving mindset. This reframing suggests that she is actively seeking meaning and lessons from her experiences rather than remaining stuck in victimhood.

Kellie's recognition that people can take different paths, regardless of the depth of their connection, shows an acceptance of life's impermanence. Her focus on building a fulfilling life without dependency reflects a sense of hope and determination to create her happiness. Despite disappointment in herself, Kellie chooses to honor and prioritize her well-being. This is a powerful declaration of self-love and commitment to personal growth.

Kellie's conflicting emotions—holding onto memories while striving to move on—highlight the duality of her experience. This internal conflict is natural in healing, as it often involves simultaneous feelings of grief for the past and hope for the future. She confronts her disappointment in herself, which adds a layer of complexity to her healing. This self-criticism could either propel her growth or hinder it if not balanced by self-compassion. Fortunately, her commitment to *self-love* suggests she is navigating this challenge constructively. By reframing her experiences as lessons rather than punishments, Kellie empowers herself. This perspective shift reduces the emotional weight of her pain and allows her to see her breakup as a catalyst for growth.

Kellie's resolve to prioritize herself and build a fulfilling life demonstrates resilience. She is not allowing her past relationship to define her future but instead uses it as motivation to achieve independence and joy. Her focus on finding fulfillment within herself rather than through others is a significant step in breaking patterns of dependency. This reflects a growing emotional maturity and self-reliance.

Kellie's journal entry is a testament to her emotional journey, marked by introspection, resilience, and the determination to heal. While she acknowledges the pain and complexity of moving on, her focus on self-love and personal growth signals a hopeful trajectory. This entry encapsulates the essence of healing—embracing the discomfort of change while striving toward a better, more fulfilling life.

Journal Entry—Day 43: Mood—uplifted, reflective, and self-affirming.

Today, I Celebrated My Small Wins. I made it a point to celebrate the progress I've been making, no matter how small—whether it's a shift in how I feel, a slight change on the scale, or simply choosing to eat healthier. These small victories remind me that slow, steady progress adds up to meaningful change.

To honor these steps forward, I treated myself to a well-deserved spa day. I packed everything I needed: swimwear, flip-flops, workout clothes, makeup, haircare essentials, toiletries, and cozy outfits. The day was an indulgence in self-care and a celebration of how far I've come. At the spa, I immersed myself in pure relaxation. First stop was for the body treatments: Sauna, whirlpool, jet bath, steam room, massage, mud bath, salt scrub, seaweed body wraps, herbal masks, reflexology, and even waxing. Then, a facial care that left my skin feeling refreshed, hydrated, and radiant. Finally, for hands and feet: A manicure, pedicure, and paraffin treatments left me feeling polished and pampered.

The experience was nothing short of amazing. Taking this time for myself reinforced how much progress I have made—emotionally, physically, and mentally—and reminded me to appreciate every step of the journey.

Self-love is a balance of discipline and indulgence. It is about staying committed to long-term goals while also pausing to reward myself for the work I've done. Today's sensory experience of relaxation was a powerful reminder of the joy in being alive, present in my body, and grateful for this life.

Celebrating small wins has become an important part of staying motivated. When I treat myself, my body and nervous system recognize the reward, and it strengthens my resolve to keep going. This spa day was not just a luxury—it was a way to honor my progress and thank myself for showing up, day by day, to create the life I want.

Reflection & Analysis: Rooted In Renewal

Kellie conveys a sense of pride in her progress, gratitude for her journey, and joy in celebrating her accomplishments. Her tone reflects a balance between recognizing the discipline and effort she has invested in her self-improvement and appreciating the sensory pleasures of self-care. There is also a deep sense of self-awareness and contentment as she acknowledges her growth emotionally, physically, and mentally.

Kellie's journal entry reflects a significant shift toward self-empowerment, self-care, and mindfulness. She emphasizes the importance of acknowledging incremental progress, both in her physical goals (e.g., changes in her health) and her emotional and mental growth. This recognition helps reinforce her commitment to her journey, providing motivation to continue. By celebrating small wins, she demonstrates an understanding of how cumulative efforts lead to meaningful change. This approach reflects a growth mindset, in which Kellie values progress over perfection. Celebrating small victories not only boosts her morale but also strengthens her ability to stay consistent and disciplined.

Kellie's detailed recounting of her spa day underscores the importance she places on self-care. The sensory experience of pampering herself is both a reward for her hard work and a way to nurture her physical and emotional well-being. The spa treatments symbolize her commitment to self-love and self-respect. This indulgence is not just about luxury but also about reconnecting with her body, calming her nervous system, and fostering gratitude for the journey she is on. It shows a holistic understanding of healing, encompassing both discipline (achieving goals) and reward (self-pampering).

Kellie notes that her body and nervous system respond to the rewards of self-care and relaxation. She connects the physiological benefits of relaxation (e.g., calming her nervous system) with the emotional and psychological reinforcement of her progress. This observation reflects a deepening awareness of the mind-body connection. Kellie recognizes that self-care practices not only enhance her physical state but also influence her mental resilience and emotional stability. This mindfulness indicates a growing sense of harmony within herself. She acknowledges that self-love involves both discipline (staying consistent with her goals) and indulgence (allowing herself to feel pampered).

She describes this duality as both "pain and pleasure," showing a nuanced understanding of the sacrifices and rewards of personal growth. This duality reveals Kellie's maturity in balancing challenging work with moments of joy and relaxation. It reflects her ability to maintain focus on long-term goals while finding fulfillment in the present.

Kellie's appreciation of her spa day highlights her capacity to be present and grateful for the moment. She acknowledges the sensations, emotions, and benefits she experiences, reinforcing a sense of joy and self-worth. This focus on gratitude and mindfulness underscores her progress in shifting from external validation to internal contentment. By being fully present, she is grounding herself in her current accomplishments rather than dwelling on past regrets or future uncertainties.

Kellie's journal entry is a celebration of transformation and resilience. She has moved from a place of self-doubt and emotional turmoil to a state of self-appreciation and empowerment. By integrating self-care, discipline, and mindfulness into her life, she is building a foundation for sustained emotional, physical, and mental well-being. Her journey illustrates the importance of celebrating progress, embracing self-love in all its forms, and staying present in the pursuit of personal growth. This entry demonstrates that Kellie is not just surviving her challenges but thriving as she discovers her capacity for resilience and joy.

Journal Entry—Day 44: Mood—a blend of introspection, determination, and triumph.

Loneliness creeps in like an uninvited guest on Friday and Saturday nights, slinking through the cracks, settling into the empty spaces of my heart. Tonight, it slithered in softly, whispering in my ear, tempting me to rekindle dying embers with an ex or swipe aimlessly through dating apps, searching for a spark. It carried the weight of hollow longing, the ache of wanting to be held, understood, seen. A quiet, gnawing void stretched inside me, echoing with the ache of companionship unmet.

I know this feeling too well. It's the same ghost that kept me tethered to past relationships, even the toxic ones. Because sometimes, the chaos of dysfunction feels easier to bear than the heavy silence of

solitude. But I've learned something—I can't fill the void with someone else's presence. To truly feel whole, I have to sit with it, breathe
through it, make peace with my own company.

My gaze landed on my laptop, its glow casting soft light into my dim
room. Among the clutter of open tabs, an event I had bookmarked
stared back at me: LA Fashion Week. A show in Hollywood. A rush
of excitement stirred somewhere deep in my chest—I had always loved
fashion. A spark, a possibility. Maybe this was my way out of tonight's
lonely grip. I picked up my phone, dialed a couple of friends, hoping
for company. No luck. Too last-minute. The idea of going alone sent
a ripple of unease through me. The drive to LA, the hunt for parking,
stepping into a buzzing Saturday night crowd—solo.

For a moment, I hesitated. Then, a challenge rose in my mind: Get
up. Get dressed. Go.

I checked for tickets—only one left. As if the universe had carved
out this moment just for me. I bought it before doubt could steal my
courage.

As I slipped into a black body-con dress, fastened a Gucci buckle
belt around my waist, and stepped into leopard-print kitten heels, a
familiar pang surfaced—memories of dressing up for Rob. The way
his eyes used to linger on me, the way I used to seek his approval. A
bittersweet sigh left my lips. But tonight, I whispered to my reflection,
a woman can get ready for herself. She can be beautiful for herself.

The drive to Hollywood felt like stepping into another version of
myself—the kind who takes chances, who dares to live for her own
pleasure. And as if the night conspired in my favor, I found myself
ushered to a VIP seat right by the runway. The air hummed with energy, a kaleidoscope of colors, sequins, and audacious designs flashing
before my eyes. I leaned in, drinking in the beauty, the artistry, the
pulse of the moment.

In between shows, I struck up conversations with strangers—fellow fashion lovers, creatives, dreamers. A photographer told me about her stunning photoshoots featuring flowing red dresses against the waves of Laguna Beach. Something in me lit up. Would I do it? The idea thrilled me. A bold, spontaneous yes slipped past my lips before fear could intervene.

Later, I let my feet wander through Hollywood, the city thrumming with life—neon lights reflecting on the pavement, music spilling from open doors, laughter weaving through the air. I stopped for a slice of New York-style Margherita pizza, savoring the warmth, the rich basil-scented bite, the way independence tasted on my tongue.

What began as a night shadowed by loneliness transformed into something luminous. I had ventured out alone and found magic waiting for me. I had built my own adventure, crafted my own joy. No partner's validation, no arm to hold—just me, in my own skin, feeling the quiet, rebellious thrill of choosing myself.

That night, I didn't just survive loneliness—I conquered it. I danced with it, outwitted it, turned it into something golden. And for the first time in a long while, I felt the pure, intoxicating joy of being free.

Reflection & Analysis: From Loneliness to Liberation

Initially, Kellie feels lonely, nostalgic, and wistful, as she struggles with emptiness and longing for companionship. However, she channels these feelings into a productive and empowering action by embracing her independence. As the night unfolds, her mood shifts to excitement, curiosity, and pride as she steps out of her comfort zone, attends the fashion show alone, and has new experiences. By the end of her journal entry, she radiates a sense of accomplishment, liberation, and self-love, having proven to herself that she can create her own happiness and thrive independently.

Kellie begins by openly acknowledging her feelings of loneliness, which are particularly intense on weekends when societal norms and personal desires for companionship are more pronounced. She also identifies the temptation to seek external validation through rekindling old relationships or using dating apps. This honesty is crucial, as it shows her awareness of the emotional triggers that can lead to self-defeating patterns. Her admission about the struggle to be her own company highlights a deeper issue many face: the discomfort of solitude and the pull toward unhealthy attachments as a coping mechanism. Kellie's understanding that tolerating toxic relationships often stems from a fear of loneliness demonstrates her growing emotional intelligence and insight into human behavior.

Faced with these emotions, Kellie chooses an active and constructive response. She recognizes that her feelings, while valid, do not have to dictate her actions. By venturing out alone to the fashion show, she challenges her own fears, builds self-reliance, and discovers the joy and freedom of independence. This decision to attend the event alone serves as a turning point. It represents her ability to reframe her narrative: instead of focusing on what she lacks (a partner), she shifts her energy toward what she can create—new experiences, connections, and memories.

The entry is infused with themes of empowerment. Kellie embraces the concept of dressing up for herself, enjoying the process of self-presentation as an act of self-love rather than for someone else's validation. Her positive encounters at the event, such as making new connections and booking a photoshoot, reinforce her sense of agency and independence. By the end of the evening, Kellie reflects on the liberation of being single and the opportunities it offers. She acknowledges that these experiences might not have been possible had she been coupled or preoccupied with someone else. This realization deepens her appreciation for her own company and the potential for personal growth in solitude. Kellie's ability to name and confront her feelings of loneliness is a significant step toward emotional healing. By stepping out of her comfort zone, she discovers new joys and connections, proving to herself that she can create her own happiness.

Kellie's experience underscores the value of independence and self-reliance, reminding us that personal fulfillment often lies within. Through this experience, Kellie strengthens her resilience, demonstrating that facing discomfort can lead to profound personal growth. Kellie's journal entry is a testament to her evolving strength, self-awareness, and commitment to building a fulfilling life on her own terms. It is an inspiring narrative of how one can confront loneliness, embrace independence, and find joy and purpose in new beginnings.

Journal Entry—Day 45: Mood—reflective and optimistic.

L ast night, venturing out to watch a fashion show, sitting among fashion elites, and witnessing the models strutting down the runway felt like a significant leap in my journey of conquering loneliness. However, the daily reality of being alone is something I continue to navigate and confront. Moments of yearning for a significant other to share the minute details of life with and to feel that connection remain challenging at times.

I have come to understand that life is, at its core, a solo experience. No matter what it looks like from the outside, whether with a significant other, surrounded by friends, or in a crowd, life comes down to how I choose to live it and the decisions I make about how to spend my time. Loneliness, I realize, is a choice, and I hold the power to address it, even in small, simple ways like moving my body, taking long walks, reading, or curating wish lists while online shopping. No one can solve this for me; it is up to me to figure it out.

As I continue healing, I'm discovering an array of interesting things to do and learn. My focus now is on making deliberate efforts to enrich my life, and without the distraction of a romantic interest at this moment, I have the space to cultivate new hobbies, set meaningful goals, and create my own joy. Silence has given me the clarity to focus inward and tune into what I genuinely want. Passively drifting through life is not an option—there's always something purposeful I can do.

In this time of self-discovery, I find myself asking: how can I satisfy my primal need for connection and intimacy without being in a relationship? The answer lies in diversifying how I connect—with others and with myself. I have been focusing on strengthening bonds with close friends through vulnerable conversations and shared experiences that foster emotional intimacy. These connections remind me that I am seen, understood, and valued.

Joining clubs, groups, or communities aligned with my interests, whether in fitness, art, or volunteering, has opened opportunities to connect with others through shared goals and passions. Activities like yoga exercise or getting pampered with massages fulfill my need for touch and physical closeness, as do platonic gestures like hugs from friends or family.

Journaling, art, and music have become powerful ways to pour out my emotions. Sharing my creations provides a sense of intimacy and connection with an audience or even my community. Practices like mindfulness and journaling help me build a deeper relationship with myself. By engaging in activities that make me feel alive, I uncover new hobbies and goals that spark joy and purpose.

Each day, I'm learning how to satisfy my innate need for intimacy in meaningful, non-romantic ways. By embracing a diverse approach to connection—both externally with others and internally with myself, I am discovering the richness and fulfillment of life on my own terms.

Reflection & Analysis: Finding Fulfillment in One-self

Kellie acknowledges feelings of loneliness and the challenges of navigating life without a romantic partner, but her tone suggests a sense of empowerment and growth. She is focused on healing, finding joy in self-discovery, and diversifying her sources of connection and intimacy. While there are moments of vulnerability and longing, they are balanced by a strong resolve to create a fulfilling and meaningful life independently. Her mood also carries a sense of hope and determination as she embraces her journey of self-development.

Kellie's journal entry reveals a deep introspection and an evolving sense of self-awareness. She reflects on her journey of healing and how she is consciously learning to address loneliness and the desire for connection in constructive and fulfilling ways. She recognizes these emotions as natural but does not allow them to dominate her actions or decisions. This acknowledgment is an essential step in processing and moving forward from these feelings. Instead of succumbing to the urge for a romantic relationship to fill the void, she is redirecting her energy toward self-discovery, personal growth, and exploring her interests. This shows maturity in her approach to dealing with emotional challenges and a commitment to creating a fulfilling life for herself.

Kellie outlines several strategies for addressing her need for intimacy and connection, such as deepening friendships, engaging in community activities, and finding comfort in physical activities like yoga and massage. This pro-active approach reflects her determination to meet her emotional needs in diverse and healthy ways. Her focus on mindfulness, journaling, and creative outlets highlights her journey toward self-connection and emotional self-sufficiency. This deepening relationship with herself forms the foundation for her ongoing healing and personal growth.

Kellie's tone conveys a sense of optimism and empowerment. She is no longer passively experiencing life but actively shaping it by making intentional choices that align with her values and goals. She recognizes her agency in creating happiness and meaning in her life. While she acknowledges the challenges and discomfort of being alone, Kellie also finds opportunities to celebrate her independence and the freedom it offers. This balanced perspective helps her to navigate difficult emotions without being overwhelmed by them. She is learning to rely on herself for fulfillment and happiness, reducing dependency on external validation or relationships and actively overcoming the instinct to cling to others for comfort and instead faces her emotions head-on.

Kellie is embracing this phase of her life as an opportunity to explore new hobbies, friendships, and personal interests, which adds richness and purpose to her journey. Kellie's journal reflects a powerful journey of self-discovery and resilience. She is learning to navigate the complexities of loneliness, not by avoiding it, but by confronting it and transforming it into an opportunity for growth. Her entry is a testament to the human capacity for adaptation and the ability to find fulfillment in oneself and in life's small yet meaningful moments.

Journal Entry—Day 46: Mood—reflective, empowered, and hopeful, with an undercurrent of melancholy.

Although I value connecting with others and recognize that relationships enrich our lives and help us navigate challenging times, I've come to appreciate the profound peace of being alone. This time of solitude has allowed me to detach from external validation and sources of happiness, turning inward to find that these qualities have always been within me. The space and silence I have embraced are gifts, offering emotional clarity and helping me process my feelings without the distractions of a past relationship or the pressure to pursue new romantic connections.

For now, this silence is a sanctuary—helping me cultivate independence, strengthen my self-esteem, and remind myself of my worth beyond romantic relationships. By giving myself this time apart and refraining from reaching out to old connections, I have found the clarity and distance necessary to focus on personal growth and set new goals. Silence has become a healing force, teaching me to trust myself and follow my instincts. Sometimes, the best way forward is to prioritize my own journey, and I am learning to do just that.

When I was with Rob, my mind was consumed with the idea of building a solid relationship. Now, I am redirecting that passion toward romanticizing my own life instead. This shift has opened my eyes to the possibilities of creating a fulfilling, exciting life that is my own, without relying on anyone else to define my happiness. This silence, this space I've created, is a gift reminder that my well-being is my top priority. Every time I choose to focus on myself instead of seeking external validation or entertaining thoughts of rekindling things with Rob, I reinforce my self-worth.

Over time, I have found peace in knowing that my value is intrinsic, not something granted by others. Happiness is not just my right; it is my responsibility. In the past, when I wasn't comfortable being alone, I sought external things to fill a void that could only be addressed from within. Now that I've provided myself with peace, I crave solitude, rest, and privacy. I cherish self-preservation, deep sleep, and the ongoing journey of self-discovery.

While part of me still feels a longing and yearning for Rob, my heart and mind firmly say no. My body echoes this sentiment—my nervous system has been calm, and I've been sleeping better than ever. The absence of anxiety and drama has brought a new level of clarity to my life. I am proud of myself for enduring and emerging from the darkness, and though the path is still unfolding, I am choosing to heal and shine.

I've committed myself to my fitness journey, sobriety, healthy eating, mental wellness, and peace. No more toxic cycles or drama from immature relationships. Looking back, I now see the toxicity I escaped, and I am grateful for the opportunity to rediscover myself. Initially, being single felt lonely and painful, but I am beginning to find it empowering.

This silence I have embraced pushes me beyond my comfort zone, introducing a new kind of freedom and fun. It has given me the space to explore my boundaries and achieve a deeper sense of accomplishment. Through this transformation, I'm choosing not to conform to old patterns but to trust myself, believe in my journey, and create a life of authenticity and self-love—all born in the quiet moments of solitude.

Reflection & Analysis: The Power of Solitude

Kellie acknowledges the lingering sadness and yearning from her past relationship but balances this with a growing sense of pride and fulfillment in her personal growth. Her tone conveys a deep introspection and self-awareness as she navigates the challenges of solitude, finding strength and empowerment in embracing her independence and focusing on her well-being.

Kellie's journal entry reveals a profound journey of self-discovery, healing, and empowerment. It offers insight into her emotional state and the steps she is taking to reclaim her sense of self after the end of a toxic relationship. Kellie acknowledges her initial discomfort with being alone and her yearning for her past relationship with Rob. Yet, she differentiates between loneliness and the intentional solitude she now embraces. This shows her growing understanding that being alone can foster self-discovery rather than merely serve as a void to be filled.

Kellie's recognition of the value of solitude reflects maturity. She reframes loneliness as an opportunity for growth, signaling a shift from dependence on external validation to inner resilience. Kellie credits silence and solitude for providing emotional clarity to process her feelings and focus on her goals. She now sees her worth outside the context of a romantic relationship, acknowledging that happiness is her responsibility. This transition marks a pivotal moment in her healing journey. By recognizing her value independent of external validation, she reclaims agency over her emotional and mental health.

Kellie finds empowerment in her fitness journey, sobriety, and commitment to healthier choices. She views these changes not as sacrifices but as acts of self-love that have strengthened her sense of identity and well-being. These positive habits signify a deeper transformation beyond just healing from a breakup. Kellie's focus on personal growth illustrates her resilience and dedication to building a fulfilling life on her terms.

Kellie explicitly rejects the toxic dynamics of her past relationship and celebrates the newfound peace in her life. She highlights the freedom from drama and anxiety, finding empowerment in her decision to remain single for the time being. Her recognition of the toxicity in her past relationship and her deliberate decision to avoid such patterns in the future underscores her commitment to self-respect and self-preservation.

Despite lingering feelings of longing and sadness, Kellie expresses gratitude for the darkness she endured, framing it as an essential part of her growth. She looks forward to continued self-discovery and transformation. This gratitude for her challenges suggests emotional resilience and a forward-looking mindset. Her optimism about her evolving identity and the possibilities ahead reinforces her ability to find purpose even in adversity.

Kellie's journal entry is a testament to her emotional strength and determination. While she still experiences moments of vulnerability, her focus on self-love, growth, and transformation demonstrates her ability to navigate those feelings constructively. Her willingness to confront discomfort and embrace solitude as a tool for healing is inspiring, serving as a reminder that personal fulfillment often begins with self-awareness and the courage to prioritize oneself.

Journal Entry—Day 47: Mood—a mix of excitement, gratitude, and disbelief, coupled with a touch of nervous anticipation.

Speaking of self-discovery, trying new things, and embracing adventure, I'm reminded of the photoshoot I recently booked with Liya, a photographer I met at the LA Fashion Week event. We struck up a conversation after she asked to take a picture of me during the show. In our brief chat, we introduced ourselves, and I learned that her studio is based in Orange County. Liya had spent over a decade in Dubai as a professional photographer before moving to California to start fresh. When she showed me her Instagram portfolio, I was blown away—her work is stunning!

During our chat, Liya mentioned a unique concept she specializes in: the "flying dress" photoshoot. It's a style she successfully executed in Dubai and now wants to bring to her clients in the U.S. Without fully thinking it through—or even asking about the cost, I excitedly agreed to book a session. Later, panic set in as I realized I might have committed to something that could break my bank! I sent her a message on Instagram to inquire about the price, bracing myself for the worst.

To my surprise, Liya responded with incredible generosity. She said not to worry about the cost because she wanted me to model for her Instagram page as part of her U.S. launch for the flying dress concept. I was stunned. I protested, explaining that I wasn't a model and had zero experience posing for professional photos. But Liya reassured me, saying she saw something in me that she believed would make the photoshoot special. Her confidence in me was both humbling and thrilling.

The photoshoot will feature a dramatic red satin dress, flowing amidst the waves at Laguna Beach. Liya explained that the dress, made of tens of yards of lightweight fabric and weighing about five pounds, will move beautifully with the ocean breeze. The motion of the wind, along with some running or flipping, will create the iconic "flying" effect. I was captivated by her vision, especially after seeing her breathtaking desert photos from Dubai. Bringing this concept to the ocean feels like a bold and creative evolution.

Liya also assured me she would have a professional crew on hand to style my hair and makeup. Every detail is being carefully planned to ensure the shoot captures the elegance and motion of the flying dress. As nervous as I feel about stepping into this role, I'm also deeply excited. This is an opportunity I never imagined for myself, a chance to express a new side of me, step out of my comfort zone, and simply have fun with an incredible experience.

I still cannot believe Liya is entrusting me to modeling her flying dress and feature me on her professional Instagram page. It is exhilarating and a bit surreal. But more than anything, I am thrilled to take on this adventure and see where it leads. Sometimes, the best opportunities are the ones you never saw coming!

Reflection & Analysis: Taking Flight: Embracing the Unexpected and Finding Freedom

Kellie is thrilled about the unexpected opportunity to model in a photoshoot, a novel and exhilarating experience for her. Her gratitude shines through as she acknowledges Liya's trust and generosity, and there is a sense of disbelief that she has been chosen for such an extraordinary role. While she initially feels a bit anxious and self-conscious about her lack of modeling experience, her excitement and willingness to embrace this adventure override her doubts. Overall, her mood is positive, buoyant, and reflective of a growing confidence in stepping outside her comfort zone.

Kellie's journal entry reflects her evolving journey of self-discovery and personal growth. Through her narrative, we see themes of unexpected opportunities, self-doubt, and the courage to embrace new experiences. Kellie is stepping into an unfamiliar world by agreeing to model for the photoshoot. This opportunity symbolizes her willingness to try something bold and new, which aligns with her broader theme of exploring life outside her comfort zone. The photoshoot, with its concept of a "flying red dress," is not just about the act itself but represents freedom, transformation, and self-expression. It is a metaphorical and literal moment of her life taking flight.

Kellie acknowledges Liya's trust in her potential, even when she doubts herself. This demonstrates her growing ability to appreciate external validation as a boost, while acknowledging her intrinsic worth. Her gratitude toward Liya and her excitement about the photoshoot highlight how she is opening herself up to new people and experiences. She openly admits her initial hesitation and nervousness about modeling. Her self-awareness and willingness to articulate these fears show emotional growth. Instead of allowing self-doubt to paralyze her, Kellie chooses to focus on the adventure and the fun that comes with it, demonstrating resilience.

The flying dress, with its flowing motion, mirrors Kellie's inner transformation. It represents the dynamic, liberating energy she is embracing in her life. By participating in the shoot, she is quite literally embodying this sense of freedom. Kellie's decision to proceed with the photoshoot is a testament to her growing confidence and openness to challenge her limits. It shows her willingness to take risks and embrace her unique journey.

Meeting Liya at the fashion show and the resulting opportunity highlights the importance of building connections. This reinforces the idea that meaningful relationships can emerge unexpectedly, adding richness and excitement to her life. This experience is another chapter in Kellie's broader narrative of self-discovery. Her reflection shows how she is intentionally seeking moments that challenge her, inspire her, and bring joy. The description of the dress and the photoshoot setting underscores the transformative and empowering nature of the moment. By embracing this opportunity, Kellie is metaphorically learning to "fly" on her own.

Kellie's journal entry is an inspiring account of stepping into the unknown with courage and grace. It reflects her journey of self-discovery and self-expression, where she is learning to embrace opportunities and trust her own potential. The experience is a celebration of growth, connection, and the joy of exploring life on her own terms.

Journal Entry—Day 48: Mood—a blend of anxiety, self-doubt, and introspection, but also includes an undercurrent of determination and a desire for self-empowerment.

L ately, I have been feeling uneasy about the upcoming red dress photoshoot. Doubts keep swirling in my mind—do I deserve to be in the spotlight or in front of the camera? A part of me wants to postpone it, thinking I might feel more confident if I lost a few more pounds or if my hair was longer. But as I dig deeper, I realize these insecurities are running far deeper than surface-level concerns.

I've done my research on Liya, the photographer, and everything about her checks out. Her Instagram is filled with remarkable work, and her experience speaks for itself. Yet, I can't seem to shake this nagging doubt—about her, the circumstances, and most of all, myself. Why do I keep finding flaws and making excuses? Why do I feel so undeserving of this opportunity?

Maybe it's because it's my first time doing something like this, or because my confidence has taken a hit after the breakup. I'm just not ready yet—still healing, still finding my footing. Or maybe this self-doubt is part of a larger pattern I've struggled with for so long. I find myself picking at every perceived imperfection, convincing myself I'm not enough. And as much as I hate to admit it, I realize I'm still seeking validation—from someone, somewhere—just to feel accepted.

This shadow of insecurity always seems to lurk nearby, whispering doubts into my ear. As I sat with these feelings, observing my thoughts, I noticed the patterns: self-doubt, overthinking, needing reassurance, and even self-sabotage. Whether it's hesitating to follow through on commitments, staying in my comfort zone, or caring too much about what others think, I see how these behaviors have held me back before. And here they are again, trying to take over something that should be exciting and celebratory.

But instead of running from these uncomfortable feelings, I chose to face them. I let myself process the discomfort and acknowledged the inner critic that keeps trying to pull me down. I reminded myself that I do not need external validation to prove my worth—I need to believe in myself, to be my own support, my own cheerleader. It is not easy, but I know I have to cultivate that inner strength if I want to grow.

This back-and-forth—the pull to cancel versus the push to be bold—feels overwhelming at times. But deep down, I know this opportunity is about more than a photoshoot. It's about stepping out of my comfort zone, quieting the self-doubt, and proving to myself that I can do this. I do not need to be "perfect." I just need to show up, flaws and all, and trust that I am enough.

Reflection & Analysis: Self Sabotaging Tendencies

Kellie feels uneasy and insecure about the photoshoot. She questions her worthiness and readiness for the opportunity, focusing on perceived flaws. She reflects deeply on the origins of her insecurities, recognizing patterns of self-sabotage, her inner demons, and the tendency to seek external validation. Kellie acknowledges her emotional struggles and overthinking tendencies.

Despite her self-doubt, she demonstrates an awareness of the need to cultivate self-belief and inner strength. She recognizes the significance of stepping out of her comfort zone and facing her fears as part of her growth journey. Kellie's mood oscillates between vulnerability and strength as she navigates her emotions, leaning toward self-acceptance and courage. Kellie's hesitation about the photoshoot reflects an internalized standard of perfection. She postpones her readiness based on physical appearance and a belief that she needs to be "more" (thinner, more confident, or experienced). This highlights the pervasive nature of self-criticism and how it can create barriers to embracing new experiences.

Kellie thoughtfully acknowledges that her lack of confidence may stem from both her recent breakup and deeper, more ingrained self-esteem issues. This awareness is a crucial step in addressing and eventually healing these wounds. Her tendency to analyze every angle, from doubting the photographer's intentions to questioning her own readiness, demonstrates overthinking as a response to vulnerability. This cycle of thought serves to protect her from perceived risks but also holds her back. Despite her struggles, Kellie recognizes the patterns of self-sabotage and the need to cultivate inner strength. Sitting with discomfort and observing her thoughts signifies her effort to process emotions rather than suppress them, showing emotional maturity.

Kellie's internal conflict highlights the tension between fear of failure and the allure of growth. The photoshoot represents more than an event; it is a metaphor for stepping into a new version of herself. Her struggle reflects a common human experience: the battle between comfort zones and aspirations. Kellie acknowledges her reliance on external validation to affirm her worth, a pattern she is trying to break. This insight demonstrates growth and a desire for self-reliance. By choosing to sit with her discomfort rather than react impulsively (canceling the shoot or seeking reassurance), Kellie is building resilience. Her awareness of behaviors like blame-shifting or avoiding challenges shows a commitment to personal accountability.

The rawness of her self-doubt makes her eventual decision to confront these fears even more significant. Her process is not linear, but she shows the courage to question negative thought patterns and seek a new narrative. Kellie's journal entry is a testament to the complexity of personal growth. It captures her vulnerability, but also her willingness to confront it. This moment of doubt is also a moment of transformation. By recognizing her self-sabotaging tendencies and choosing to lean into discomfort, Kellie is building the foundation for greater confidence and self-assuredness. Her journey is not just about the photoshoot but about redefining how she sees herself and her capabilities.

Journal Entry—Day 49: Mood—amazement and pride; empowerment and transformation.

The ocean air kissed my skin as I stepped into Liya's studio in Laguna Beach, a sun-drenched haven perched above the Pacific. Soft white curtains swayed in the salty breeze, filtering golden light that bathed the space in an ethereal glow. The scent of fresh coffee mingled with the ocean's breath, and a melodic hum of music played in the background, setting the stage for something that felt almost otherworldly.

Joey, the makeup artist, welcomed me with a warm smile, leading me to a well-lit vanity lined with an array of beauty essentials—glistening palettes, delicate brushes, sleek tubes of color. Beside him, Diane, the hairstylist, arranged her collection of curling irons and sprays, her fingers already itching to transform me. Liya, the mastermind behind it all, moved with effortless grace, adjusting her camera, fine-tuning the details of her vision, and casting knowing glances my way, as if she saw something in me that I had yet to discover.

Joey's hands worked like an artist's brush on a canvas, sweeping soft, featherlight strokes across my skin. As he blended warm hues and sculpted my features, he talked about the magic of transformation—the way makeup was not about covering up but rather revealing the essence of someone's inner light. When he finally reached for the red lipstick, he paused, grinning. "This," he said, "is going to change everything."

Diane followed, her fingers weaving through my hair, teasing it into bold, voluminous curls. "Goddess energy," she whispered as she worked. I closed my eyes, allowing myself to surrender to their artistry, to the sensation of being cared for, celebrated. This was more than preparation, it was a ritual. A rebirth.

Then, Liya unveiled the dress.

A river of crimson satin cascaded from her hands, rippling like liquid fire in the sunlight. It was breathtaking—dramatic, daring, undeniably powerful. My breath caught in my throat as she draped it over me, fastening it with careful hands. The fabric clung to my frame, pooling at my feet like a statement, a declaration.

"Look," Liya urged.

I turned to the mirror—and time seemed to still.

The woman staring back at me was mesmerizing. Not just beautiful—powerful. A force. My heart pounded at the unfamiliar sight of myself, wrapped in boldness, exuding a confidence I had never fully claimed. Joey let out a low whistle. Diane beamed. Liya simply nodded, as if she had always known this version of me existed.

In that moment, I understood. This wasn't just a photoshoot. It was an awakening.

We drove to Main Beach, where the world shimmered in a way that felt surreal—the sky an endless canvas of blue, the waves roaring their approval. As we walked, heads turned, strangers pausing to take in the sight of the woman in the flowing red dress. For a fleeting moment, I felt like a star, radiating a kind of untouchable magic.

At the shore, Liya directed me onto a sun-warmed rock, positioning me against the rhythmic crash of the waves. "Let the wind take it," she instructed. And then, the ocean exhaled. The fabric lifted, twisting and billowing around me like flames caught in a storm. Liya's camera clicked in rapid succession, capturing the dance of silk and wind, the raw, unfiltered moment of movement and emotion. I tilted my chin higher, let the dress take flight, let myself take flight.

The crowd watching from the sidelines blurred into nothing. There was only the pulse of the moment—the energy, the liberation, the sheer exhilaration of surrendering to something greater than myself. The camera continued to snap, and with each frame, I felt my inhibitions shedding, my doubts dissolving.

By the end, Liya grinned. "You looked like you were made for this."

And maybe I was.

As I stood there, toes sinking into the cool sand, the red dress draped around me like a whisper of everything I had just discovered, I realized this had never been about looking beautiful in photographs. It was about seeing myself—truly seeing myself—as bold, breathtaking, and unafraid.

This was not just a photoshoot. This was proof.

Proof that I was no longer waiting for life to happen to me.

I was happening to life.

And it was beautiful.

Reflection & Analysis: Transformation & Self-Discovery

The passage is rich with sensory detail, making the experience feel almost cinematic. The ocean air, golden light, and flowing red satin create an atmosphere that feels both ethereal and grounded in reality. Each of these elements serves as a metaphor: The ocean represents freedom, vastness, and the unknown—a force that mirrors Kellie's own growth. The red dress symbolizes power, passion, and a declaration of self-assurance. It isn't just a garment; it's a transformation, wrapping her in confidence and commanding attention.

The wind lifting the fabric parallels Kellie's own emotional release, her ability to surrender to the moment and embrace who she truly is. At the heart of this journal entry is Kellie's realization that beauty isn't just about how she looks but about how she sees herself. The moment she turns to the mirror is pivotal: "Not just beautiful—powerful. A force." This is a turning point where she recognizes her own strength.

The reactions of Joey, Diane, and Liya serve as validation—not of external beauty, but of the powerful presence they always saw in her. The photoshoot itself becomes a metaphor for stepping into her own light. The act of being captured by the camera isn't about performance but about proof—proof that she is bold, fearless, and fully present in her own life.

"I was no longer waiting for life to happen to me. I was happening to life."

This statement marks a complete shift in mindset. Where once Kellie may have been hesitant or unsure, she now claims her own narrative. She moves from being passive to active, from self-doubt to self-ownership. Kellie's journal entry is more than a recollection—it is a testament to personal growth. It is about stepping out of the shadows of hesitation and fully embracing the person she was meant to be. The passage is poetic, vivid, and deeply moving, capturing a moment of pure liberation.

Ultimately, this isn't just about a red dress or a photoshoot. It's about the undeniable, exhilarating realization that she is powerful, worthy, and unstoppable.

Journal Entry—Day 50: Mood— a mix of empowerment, pride, and introspection with moments of temptation and resolve.

Today, I received an email from Liya letting me know she had completed the final edits and selected 45 of the best photos from my flying red dress photoshoot. She shared a Google Photos link with me and asked for my permission to post three of the images on her Instagram and collaborate on the post.

When I clicked the link, I could not believe my eyes. The photos captured a unique and magical experience—wearing a long, flowing red dress designed to catch the wind, creating a dramatic, elegant effect. The high-sheen satin fabric of the dress shimmered in the sunlight, and its graceful movements against the breeze added a sense of glamour and empowerment to each shot.

Some of my favorite poses included: Striking a confident stance with my hand on my waist; lifting my chin, embracing the breeze; closing my eyes with a serene smile; and extending one arm gracefully as the dress flowed around me. When Liya tagged me in the Instagram post featuring the photos, my phone started buzzing with notifications. Within hours, the post had over 3,000 likes, more engagement than I had ever received on social media. The outpouring of positivity—likes, comments, and DMs from friends and strangers alike—was overwhelming and heartwarming.

Later that afternoon, Liya called to congratulate me on the success of the photoshoot. She was thrilled about launching this unique photography concept in California, inspired by similar shoots in Greece, Dubai, Tulum, and Italy. She thanked me for being part of the debut and shared how much she admired the energy and confidence I brought to the project.

As I reflected on the experience, I felt proud and empowered. The photos weren't just beautiful, they were a celebration of my transformation, both inside and out. For a fleeting moment, I thought about sending one of the pictures to Rob as a way of making him realize what he had lost. The temptation lingered, but I wrestled with the idea and let it go.

Sending Rob the photo would have been about seeking validation, but I realized that this journey was not about him. It was about me—about reclaiming my self-worth, celebrating my growth, and honoring how far I've come. The photo is a testament to the strength I have built, physically, emotionally, and spiritually.

Rob's decision to distance himself during our relationship revealed where his priorities lay, and I've grown beyond the need for his recognition or approval. While I still think about him occasionally, I understand that those feelings stem from unresolved emotions rather than a genuine desire to reconnect.

This photoshoot is my victory. It symbolizes the self-respect and resilience I've cultivated through hard work and healing. If Rob were to see the pictures, he might notice the external changes, but he would not grasp the depth of my internal growth. I have realized I could never fully trust someone who once made me question my worth.

Instead of resisting my lingering feelings, I now accept them without judgment. Feeling longing is not a weakness, it's a reflection of my capacity for love and depth. Acknowledging these emotions without self-criticism allows me to honor my journey and stay true to myself.

This photo, this moment, this transformation—it's all for me. I've learned that my worth is not defined by someone else's validation, especially not from someone who failed to honor and respect me. Today, I stand empowered, confident, and free.

Reflection & Analysis: Personal Growth & Healing

Kellie is reflective and self-aware, experiencing a deep sense of accomplishment and growth after the photoshoot while acknowledging and processing lingering emotions tied to her past relationship. She feels proud of her transformation, celebrating her strength and newfound confidence through the success of the photoshoot and the positive feedback it generated. Kellie also grapples with a fleeting temptation to seek validation from her ex but chooses to honor her journey instead.

Kellie is deeply introspective, analyzing her emotional progress and the reasons behind her lingering thoughts about Rob. She shows a profound acceptance of her feelings without self-criticism and reaffirms her self-worth as independent of others' opinions or recognition. Overall, Kellie's mood reflects a powerful blend of self-empowerment, reflection, and emotional maturity, underpinned by her commitment to personal growth and healing.

Kellie's journal entry offers a rich narrative of personal growth, emotional introspection, and the complexities of self-worth. It reflects her journey toward empowerment, as well as her efforts to reconcile lingering emotional ties to her past. Kellie's description of the photoshoot and the positive reception of the photographs highlights her pride in the progress she has made, both externally and internally. She recognizes her transformation as a multifaceted achievement, encompassing physical, emotional, and spiritual dimensions. This moment symbolizes a significant milestone in her journey of self-discovery. It highlights her ability to celebrate herself, even amidst underlying insecurities.

Kellie's temptation to send the photo to Rob reveals a lingering connection to her past relationship. She considers the potential validation it might bring, yet refrains, recognizing the importance of preserving her progress. This internal conflict underscores her journey from seeking external validation to affirming her self-worth independently. The temptation serves as a reminder of the residual effects of a relationship that once diminished her confidence, but her resolve to prioritize her growth is a testament to her emotional maturity.

Throughout the entry, Kellie explores the deeper motivations behind her thoughts and feelings. She acknowledges the complexity of missing someone while understanding that it doesn't necessarily equate to wanting them back. This introspection is a hallmark of emotional intelligence. Kellie's ability to sit with her emotions without judgment demonstrates her capacity to heal and grow, even as she navigates unresolved feelings.

Kellie reflects on Rob's behavior in the relationship and concludes that rekindling any connection would not align with her current values or self-respect. She notes that her transformation transcends physical appearance, emphasizing her internal growth. This signifies a powerful rejection of old patterns that undermined her self-esteem. By focusing on her newfound strength, Kellie reaffirms her commitment to moving forward rather than dwelling on the past.

Kellie frames the photoshoot as a celebration of her journey, rather than a tool for seeking validation from someone who failed to honor her worth. She asserts her independence and resilience, choosing to honor her achievements for herself. This narrative shift—from seeking external approval to embracing self-celebration—marks a pivotal moment in her healing process. It reflects a deep sense of empowerment and self-ownership.

Kellie's journal entry is a testament to the resilience of the human spirit and the complexity of healing. It highlights the importance of acknowledging and accepting emotions while choosing actions that align with one's values and growth. Her decision to celebrate the photoshoot as a personal achievement, rather than a tool for external validation, demonstrates a significant step toward self-love and independence.

The entry reflects a nuanced understanding of relationships, self-worth, and the journey to empowerment, making it an inspiring narrative of transformation and resilience. Kellie's reflections serve as a powerful reminder that healing is not linear, but with self-awareness, self-compassion, and determination, it is possible to transcend past pain and create a fulfilling present.

Journal Entry—Day 51: Mood—a mix of empowerment, pride, and resilience.

My DMs were flooded with hearts, fire, and shock emojis after the pictures were posted. One of my girlfriends was shocked at my transformation. "Wow, girl, you look amazing!" she exclaimed. Another friend called and said, "Wow, incredible glow up, Kellie! Share some of your glow up tips, please?" I explained that while the heartbreak from the breakup played a role, I channeled the pain into taking better care of myself. The frustration and heartache were poured into sweat-filled yoga sessions, discipline, eating health, sobriety, and consistency of showing up for myself.

The shock and admiration from my friends were gratifying, but I told them that I appreciate the kind words while acknowledging that

I'm still working on progress. I have learned to strive for better and will always work toward becoming the best version of myself. This is a promise I have made—to remain resilient and remember that my happiness depends on me.

Life is tough, and I have faced the emotional battlefield of loss. But I am learning to fight for my joy, to earn it by resisting negative self-judgment and strengthening my mind, body, and soul. The breakup, painful as it was, became the catalyst for me to reconnect with myself and rediscover self-love.

I also understand now that life will always present setbacks. Things won't always go my way, but I have what it takes to endure. I embrace the grind, push myself, and wake up every day with a conqueror's mindset. While the external transformation is evident through the success of the photoshoot, what truly matters to me is the internal journey.

This journey has been about conquering my inner conflicting behaviors—self-doubt, insecurities, and self-sabotage—and learning to lean on myself when the man I once adored left me broken. The physical transformation is a bonus, but the resilience I've cultivated is my real triumph.

People said I'm "on fire," and perhaps that's true in more ways than one. I've reclaimed my power by focusing on what's best for me, no longer wasting time asking why it happened but instead reflecting on what I've learned. I have discovered that overcoming adversity means forging my own path with fire and ferocity, and for that, I'm proud.

Reflection & Analysis: Triumph Over Adversity

While there is an undertone of reflection on past pain and heartbreak, the predominant mood is one of self-acknowledgment and triumph over adversity. She feels proud of her physical transformation and emotional growth, and her words convey a sense of personal strength and determination to continue striving for self-improvement. Additionally, Kellie's mood reveals a sense of clarity and acceptance. She acknowledges the challenges she has faced, appreciates the positive feedback she is received, and expresses gratitude for the lessons learned through her journey. Despite some lingering reflections on her past relationship, she exhibits a keen sense of independence and empowerment in her resolve to focus on her happiness and well-being.

Kellie's journal entry is a powerful testament to her personal growth and emotional resilience. It captures the intersection of external validation and internal transformation, offering deep insights into her journey of self-discovery and empowerment. Kellie recognizes that the pain from her breakup functioned as a catalyst for notable change in her life. Instead of succumbing to negativity, she channeled her heartbreak into physical, emotional, and spiritual growth. It reflects a "phoenix rising" narrative where she rebuilt herself stronger from a place of loss and despair.

Kellie's decision to focus on self-discipline, consistency, and resilience highlights her journey toward self-reliance. She explicitly states that her happiness depends on herself, demonstrating a mature and empowering mindset. Her transformation is framed as not merely physical but deeply internal, showcasing a sense of reclaiming her power and identity.

Kellie places a high value on the internal changes she has undergone, such as overcoming self-doubt, insecurities, and self-sabotaging tendencies. This reflects emotional intelligence and a focus on mean-ingful, lasting growth rather than surface-level achievements. While she appreciates and enjoys the external validation from friends and social media, Kellie consciously reframes these accolades as secondary to her internal journey. She emphasizes the importance of conquering her inner conflicting behaviors over merely being admired for her appearance.

Kellie acknowledges the breakup as a pivotal moment in her life. Instead of dwelling on the pain or blaming external circumstances, she focuses on the lessons it taught her and the strength she gained. She expresses gratitude for her ability to persevere and for the growth the experience has brought her.

Kellie's words illustrate a growth-oriented perspective. She recog-nizes that setbacks are inevitable but believes in her ability to push through challenges and emerge stronger. Her focus on reclaiming her power, rather than lamenting her past relationship, underscores a narrative of self-empowerment. She no longer seeks validation from her ex-partner or others but has found strength within herself. Rather than dismissing her pain or treating her physical transformation as superficial, Kellie integrates both into a cohesive understanding of her journey. This integration signals emotional maturity and an integrated approach to personal development.

While Kellie exhibits strength and empowerment, there is a hint of vulnerability in her reflections. She acknowledges the temptation to seek revenge or validation from her ex, demonstrating that healing is an ongoing process, not an instantaneous achievement.

Kellie's journal entry is a celebration of resilience, self-discovery, and transformation. It is an inspiring account of how adversity can be a powerful teacher, guiding individuals toward growth and empow-erment. Her ability to focus on inner strength, while still appreciating external achievements, reflects a balanced and deeply introspective mindset. Her journey serves as a reminder that true self-worth comes from within and that overcoming challenges often leads to greater clarity, confidence, and personal fulfillment.

Journal Entry—Day 52: Mood—empowered, introspective, and resolute.

For now, silence has been my greatest refuge, a sanctuary where I can focus on my own needs and continue the journey of healing. I refuse to let anyone compromise my self-worth again. I am still healing, and in this process, I am choosing peace—no drama, just distance, silence, self-respect, and success.

I will not return to the toxic cycle of waiting, wondering, and compromising my value for the sake of someone else. I will not endure relationships that trigger insecurities, make me question if I am enough, or force me to contort myself into a mold just to be chosen. Instead, I choose myself.

As Margaret Atwood said, "The desire to be loved is the last illusion: give it up, and you will be free." I am learning to release the need to belong to someone or to seek fulfillment in partnership. That longing is born of attachment and societal expectations, but in truth, I am whole on my own. I deserve to enjoy this moment fully, for myself.

Cultivating inner confidence means celebrating my achievements, validating my joys, and taking full ownership of my life. It means allowing myself to feel every emotion fully, rather than numbing or avoiding discomfort. It is within this discomfort that I rebuild, reclaim, and rediscover myself. Shifting the focus from pain to self-love is a transformative act.

This is my time to set new goals, explore who I am without anyone else, and reclaim my independence and joy. It's okay—I simply forgot who I was for a while. Now, I am welcoming myself back.

I am so incredibly proud of myself for enduring the darkness and for choosing to heal and shine despite it all. Through every struggle, I have emerged stronger, and this journey has reminded me of my resilience.

Reflection & Analysis: Embracing Independence

Kellie is reclaiming her independence and self-worth, actively choosing herself over toxic cycles and external validation. She reflects pride in her journey of healing and transformation, which reinforces her inner strength and resilience. She is deeply reflective, examining the lessons learned from past pain and how societal norms and personal insecurities shaped her previous choices. Her thoughts on emotions, discomfort, and self-discovery show a thoughtful, self-aware mindset.

There is a firm determination in her tone to not return to old patterns that compromised her well-being. She is committed to continuing her healing process, setting new goals, and embracing her individuality with confidence. Kellie's mood conveys a sense of growth, maturity, and unwavering focus on her personal journey of self-love and empowerment. Reflecting on and analyzing Kellie's journal entry reveals a significant journey of personal growth and self-discovery.

Kellie's reflections showcase her progression from a place of emotional vulnerability to a state of empowerment: She recognizes the toxicity of previous patterns, such as waiting for validation or compromising her self-worth, and firmly commits to not revisiting those dynamics. By quoting Margaret Atwood, reflecting on societal norms around love, and belonging, Kellie affirms her intrinsic value and independence. Kellie embraces the importance of sitting with discomfort, using it as a tool for personal growth. This willingness to confront her emotions highlights her emotional resilience.

Kellie's words convey a reclaiming of power: She explicitly chooses her own well-being over external validation, signifying a transformative shift in priorities. By celebrating her perseverance through darkness, Kellie reframes her struggles as milestones in her path toward strength and healing. Kellie critiques societal pressures to seek completion in partnerships, instead embracing the idea that she is whole on her own. This introspection reflects a mature understanding of the external forces that have influenced her self-perception. She acknowledges the difficulty of her journey but also takes pride in her ability to heal and thrive. Her focus on setting new goals and embracing her independence demonstrates forward momentum and a refusal to dwell on past pain.

Kellie's journal reflects a deep emotional intelligence and a commitment to ongoing growth. She has successfully transitioned from a place of questioning her worth to recognizing her inherent value and embracing her independence. By focusing on self-respect and personal development, she sets a powerful example of resilience and empowerment.

Journal Entry—Day 53: Mood—calm, reflective, and empowered.

The peace I feel in this moment is a victory all its own—a testament to every small, deliberate choice I've made to reclaim myself. It didn't come easily. Putting myself first wasn't always comfortable, but neither was losing myself to the expectations of others. I have learned that healing isn't about grand gestures—it's about the quiet, uncelebrated moments of courage. The ones no one sees. The ones where I choose myself, even when it hurts.

Confidence isn't about having all the answers; it's about taking one step at a time, even when the path is unclear. It's about breaking free from the weight of comparison, celebrating my own progress, and recognizing my worth without waiting for external validation. There was a time when I measured myself against others, but now, I measure myself against who I used to be. That's the only comparison that matters.

Embracing vulnerability has cracked me wide open, but in the best way. Writing has become more than an outlet—it's a mirror, reflecting back the truths I once buried. Through journaling, I have learned to sit with my emotions instead of running from them. I've discovered that self-care isn't just about routines; it's about radical self-respect. Moving my body, feeding it well, allowing it to rest—these are all love letters to the person I am becoming.

But perhaps the most profound lesson of all has been the power of silence. Silence is not emptiness; it is space—space to heal, to breathe, to listen to myself without the noise of expectation. In the past, I would have rushed to defend, explain, or prove myself. Now, I understand that walking away from conflict is not weakness. It is a refusal to keep setting myself on fire to keep others warm.

Silence is my boundary. It is my declaration that I no longer participate in cycles that drain me. It is not about indifference or revenge; it is about protecting my peace. There were moments when I wanted to lash out, to respond, to make my pain understood. But I chose differently. And in that choice, I found a strength more potent than any words I could have spoken.

For me, silence is not passive—it is powerful. It is an act of self-love. It is me choosing myself over and over again, not to be better than anyone else, but to be better than the version of me who once settled for less. It is about breaking free from the weight of rejection, self-doubt, and past hurts.

This isn't about becoming someone new. It's about returning to myself—the self I was before the world told me who to be. And if there's one thing I know for sure, it's this: the most important relationship I will ever have is the one I build with myself. So I choose her. Every single day.

Reflection & Analysis: The Power of Choosing Myself

At its core, Kellie's entry is about self-empowerment through intentionality. She acknowledges that the peace she now experiences is not an accident but a product of conscious effort—daily decisions to prioritize her well-being. Her journey was not marked by grand transformations but by subtle, often painful moments of courage. This highlights the importance of consistency in healing, reinforcing the idea that true change happens in the unseen moments, in the decisions made when no one is watching.

She challenges conventional notions of confidence, shifting the focus from external validation to internal self-measurement. The comparison trap is a theme many struggle with, yet Kellie has moved beyond it, redefining success as personal growth rather than competition. Her words reflect an evolution in self-awareness—an understanding that validation must come from within.

Kellie's embrace of vulnerability is one of the most striking aspects of her reflection. She describes writing as a mirror, revealing the hidden truths she once buried. This speaks to the transformative nature of self-expression, where journaling becomes both a tool for self-discovery and a method of emotional release. Her experience echoes a broader truth: vulnerability, though often uncomfortable, is where deep healing takes root.

Perhaps the most profound realization in her journey is the recognition of silence as power. Kellie reframes silence—not as weakness, avoidance, or indifference—but as an intentional boundary. In a world that often equates silence with submission, she reclaims it as a tool for self-preservation. Her refusal to engage in draining conflicts reflects emotional maturity and self-control, reinforcing the idea that walking away can be an act of strength rather than surrender.

This newfound understanding of silence as a choice rather than a reaction is pivotal. She no longer needs to explain, justify, or defend herself—she simply chooses herself. This shift marks a deep transformation from external dependence to inner sovereignty.

Kellie's journey is not about reinvention but rediscovery. She is not becoming someone new; she is peeling away the layers of conditioning, expectations, and past wounds to return to her most authentic self. Her conclusion—"the most important relationship I will ever have is the one I build with myself"—is a powerful reminder that self-love is not a destination but a daily commitment.

This journal entry is more than a personal reflection; it is an anthem of self-liberation. Kellie's words serve as a reminder that healing is not linear, confidence is not about external validation, and silence—when chosen deliberately—can be the loudest declaration of self-worth. Her journey is one of raw honesty, resilience, and, most importantly, freedom.

Fast Forward Six Months Later: I Chose Myself, and That Changed Everything

I never thought I'd get here. Six months ago, when Rob walked away and left me in silence, I thought the quiet would swallow me whole. But instead, I let it rebuild me. I did not beg. I did not chase. I did not try to remind him of my worth—I reminded myself. And now, as I sit here reflecting, I see the undeniable proof of how far I have come.

Then: When I Was with Rob

I lived for his validation. His attention determined my worth, his words cut deep, and when he called me chubby, the wound lingered longer than it should have. I numbed my discomfort with distractions—overeating, skipping workouts, drinking to silence the doubts I refused to face. My finances spiraled; debt piled up, and bills went unpaid. My home mirrored my mind—cluttered, chaotic, neglected. I barely slept, tangled in self-doubt and the weight of what I wasn't.

Now: Six Months Later

I walked away without a word. No desperate texts, no pleading calls, no attempts to make him see what he lost. Instead, I turned inward and did the work.

Therapy became my anchor. My therapist told me I was handling the breakup in the healthiest way possible—no spiraling, no self-destruction, just healing.

Yoga became my sanctuary. I showed up, week after week, discovering a strength I never knew I had. Today, my instructor said I held my poses with power. And I felt it, too.

I changed my diet—not for appearance, but for myself. High-protein meals, intentional choices, a balance that fuels me instead of drains me. The results? I've lost weight, gained strength, and stunned my doctor with my latest blood test. I am no longer pre-diabetic. My cholesterol is perfect.

I stopped drinking. No more numbing, no more running. Six months sober, and I've never felt more in control. I take my vitamins, I nourish my body, I listen when it needs rest.

My finances? No longer a source of anxiety. I caught up on car payments, set a plan for my debt, and stopped reckless spending. My home reflects my peace now—decluttered, refreshed, intentional. I even hired a cleaning service to reset my space, and for the first time in a long time, my surroundings feel like me.

I sleep. Deep, undisturbed, and free from the noise of regret

Rob's Return—And My Choice to Stay Gone

Rob has reached out. Small, meaningless messages—breadcrumbs meant to test my feelings. I've responded, but only with grace. Neutral. Brief. I don't need to be cruel; I just need to be firm.

He knows now that the woman he walked away from no longer exists. Whether he realizes what he lost is not my concern. The truth is, love that crumbles under pressure is not the love I deserve. His departure over something as superficial as my appearance revealed his shallowness, not my shortcomings.

And while there are moments I feel a quiet longing for him, I no longer mistake it for a reason to return. I am capable of deep love, but I will never again pour it into hands that cannot hold it. I don't fight my feelings; I honor them, journal through them, and let them move through me without attachment.

I have dismantled the illusion of who Rob was in my mind. I no longer romanticize the good and ignore the ways he fell short, especially when I needed love, not judgment. That clarity has freed me.

Reclaiming My Power, Redefining My Future

Since the breakup, I have achieved more than I ever thought possible. My growth, my healing, my transformation—none of it was for him. It was for me.

Letting go doesn't mean forgetting. It means releasing myself from the grip of the past. It means making space for the love I truly deserve—one built on respect, depth, and unwavering presence. I will no longer accept love that requires me to prove my worth. The right person will see it without needing a reminder.

Rob's inability to see my value says everything about him and nothing about me. I am no longer defined by rejection, empty promises, or potential that never materialized. I honor actions, not words. And above all, I honor myself.

For now, my focus is me. My growth, my healing, my peace. I no longer seek validation outside of myself because I have reclaimed my power. Every ounce of emotional energy I once poured into a failing relationship, I now pour into becoming the woman I was always meant to be.

I have learned to say no—to people, to situations, to anything that does not align with my peace. I have forgiven Rob, but not for him. I forgave him to free myself. Resentment only anchors me to the past, and I refuse to live there. Letting go of him does not invalidate my love; it affirms my love for myself.

This journey has been brutal, beautiful, messy, and victorious. But most of all, it has been mine.

I am my own source of love, care, and validation. I am not waiting for the right partner—I am the right partner for myself. When the time comes, the right person will meet me in my wholeness, not my wounds.

For now, I am relishing the freedom, the independence, the sheer power of being my own home.

I am whole. I am enough. I am proof that even the most painful endings can be the beginning of something extraordinary.

And I will keep moving forward—because the best version of me is already here.

Final Post Break Up Journal Entry

A   **Love Once Held, A Love Reclaimed**

I find myself drifting back to the quiet moments—the ones that made love feel like home. The ones that linger, warm and familiar, long after they've passed. Rob would cook for us, his passion evident in the way he taught me to cut broccoli into perfect symmetry, how he meticulously prepared garnishes for the steak. I can still see us curled up on the couch, balancing dinner trays, Netflix humming in the background as I rested my head against his chest. His warmth, steady and familiar, lulled me into the kind of peace that felt safe.

There were nights when we'd slip into the pool under a full moon, the water wrapping around us as our conversations floated between us like drifting embers. I remember the way he was always waiting for me after a long trip, dinner ready, calling me Princess with that easy charm. The time my tea kettle sprung a leak and, instead of letting me replace it, he fixed it himself—small, thoughtful gestures that once felt like love.

He wasn't much of a dancer, but when music filled the room, I would pull him up anyway. He would blush, embarrassed by his own rhythm, but he'd indulge me, letting me sway against him. Those moments made me smile. When my dog, Bailey, was sick, he held me through my worry. And when we read together, hands intertwined, in the stillness of a quiet evening, it felt like love in its purest form—uncomplicated, present, enough.

One of my most cherished memories is the Sunday he surprised me by coming to mass with me at the basilica in San Juan Capistrano. Afterward, we spent the day wrapped in nothing but ease—brunching, watching a movie, laughing over something small but unforgettable. I still hear the echoes of our banter, the way joy came so naturally then. We watched the solar eclipse together, too, marveling at the universe, sharing a connection that felt infinite in the moment.

But love is not always enough to keep people from slipping away.

I have come to accept that it is okay to miss someone and still put yourself first. Missing Rob does not make me weak. It does not erase my progress. It does not mean I belong in the past. Instead of running from the ache, I hold space for it. Love, even when it ends, does not have to weigh you down—it can be a bridge back to yourself.

Rather than lingering in what-ifs, I choose gratitude. That love, fleeting yet beautiful, was real. And in its aftermath, I have learned what it means to choose myself. The silence that followed was not empty—it was transformative. It gave me space to breathe, to reflect, to reclaim the parts of me I once set aside.

There was a time I forgot my own strength. I poured so much of myself into proving my worth that I didn't realize I was enough all along. I bent, I stretched, I gave—without ever asking if I was receiving the same in return. Love should not require you to shrink yourself to fit inside it.

Now, as I step into my home, Bailey greets me with his familiar, boundless joy. My plants—lush monstera, cascading heartleaf philo-dendron, serene peace lilies, resilient snake plants—thrive in the quiet of my space, growing in the same light that now nurtures me. When I pull back the curtains, the Pacific Ocean stretches before me, vast and endless. The waves dance beneath the sunlight, whispering their familiar rhythm—sometimes turbulent, sometimes still, but always moving forward.

And so am I.

There is a deep peace in the life I have built—the career I have worked for, the independence I have reclaimed, the quiet I have come to cherish. I am no longer the woman I was when that love ended. I am stronger, more whole, more me. If love finds me again, it will not be because I need it to feel complete. It will be because it fits within the life I have already made beautiful.

Not every love story ends with forever, but each one leaves behind something valuable. This love, though it did not last, shaped me. And yet, it is no longer the center of my story.

I stand here now, content in my own company, surrounded by love—the love of my dog, the love of my home, the love I have poured back into myself. There are days when I still feel the ache, but it is softer now. No longer a burden, but a memory that reminds me of how deeply I have loved and how fully I have healed.

Healing is not about erasing the past. It is about making peace with it. It is about learning to hold both love and loss in the same breath and knowing that neither defines you.

I am my own home. My happiness is my own to create.

And that, I have come to understand, is the greatest love of all.

Epilogue

Looking Back with Clarity.

As I close this chapter of my life, I do so not with bitterness or regret, but with a quiet, steady gratitude. I carry no anger, only clarity. No resentment, only understanding. The silence that once felt unbearable became my sanctuary, a space where I could finally hear my own voice again. In the stillness, I found the truth that had always been there, waiting beneath the noise—I was never incomplete, never lacking, never unworthy. My worth was never something to be given or taken away; it was mine all along.

Choosing no contact was not an act of surrender—it was an act of self-respect. It was an act of love. Love for the woman who had spent too long trying to prove she was enough. Love for the person I was becoming, the one who deserved to be chosen—by me. Walking away was not easy. It was not painless. It required a kind of courage I had never known before—the courage to sit in my own company, to face the wounds I had ignored, to stop seeking comfort in the very thing that had caused my pain.

In those first weeks of silence, there were moments that ached, moments when I wanted to reach for my phone, to send a message, to seek closure that I now know would never have been enough. But each day that I stayed the course, each journal entry where I poured my heart onto the page, each sunrise where I chose myself again and again—it all brought me closer to the woman I was always meant to be.

Healing is not about erasing the past, nor is it about pretending it never mattered. It is about integrating it—taking the lessons, the love, the pain, and weaving them into the fabric of who you are. The memories, once sharp and jagged, have softened into wisdom, into gratitude. I have learned that I can miss something and still move forward. I can honor what once was without longing for its return. And I can let go—not because I am trying to forget, but because I am making space for something greater.

No contact was never just about silence. It was about reclaiming my voice. It was about breaking free from cycles that no longer served me. It was about stepping into my own power, not waiting for someone else to validate my worth, not waiting for love to arrive before I allowed myself to feel whole. It was about understanding that my happiness, my fulfillment, my peace—these are not things that exist outside of me. They are treasures I carry within myself.

And this realization changed everything.

I have seen how easily one can lose oneself in the pursuit of love. To believe that if you just give more, love harder, prove your worth a little louder, you will finally be chosen. But love—true, lasting love—is never built on proving. It is built on mutual respect, on kindness, on the simple but powerful decision to show up for each other, again and again. Love that must be fought for, begged for, earned—it was never love to begin with.

I am no longer the woman I was when that love ended. I have shed the version of me that needed to be chosen. I have become someone I am proud of. Someone who does not settle for the bare minimum, who does not twist herself into smaller versions just to fit inside someone else's world. Someone who knows her worth, not because someone told her, but because she finally sees it for herself.

And if love finds me again, it will not be because I need it to complete me. It will be because it fits within the life I have already made beautiful.

To those reading this—whether you are in the thick of heartache or just beginning to find your way back to yourself—I hope you know this: you are enough. You always have been. May you have the courage to sit with your pain, the wisdom to learn from it, and the grace to choose yourself, even when it feels like the hardest thing to do. Healing is not a straight path, but it is a worthy one. And every step you take brings you closer to the life, the love, the peace that you deserve.

The end of one story is never the end of your journey. It is the beginning of something new—something extraordinary.

So here's to endings that lead to beautiful beginnings. Here's to reclaiming your power. And here's to the greatest love story of all—the one you write with yourself.

With love and hope,

—*Kellie*

FAREWELL

"Great is the art of beginning, but greater is the art of ending."
– Henry Wadsworth Longfellow
Au revoir; Adiós; Auf Wiedersehen; Addio; Adeus; Zài jiàn; Sayōnara;
Do svidaniya; Annyeonghi gaseyo; Hoşça ka; Ma'a as-salama; Alvida;
Paalam; Shalom; Namaste; Tchau; Vale; Selamt tinggal; Le revedere;
Farvel; Moce; Zbogom; Kwaheri
Good-bye

If you made it this far, thank you. Truly.

This book was born from silence, but it ends with connection. I created something special for you—a free healing gift to walk with as you reclaim your power.

Visit: www.sagecharie.com to claim it.

If *Anatomy of No Contact* spoke to your soul, I'd be deeply grateful if you shared your thoughts in a review on Amazon, Bookbub, and Goodreads. Your words matter more than you know. Review helps this message reach more women who may feel alone in their healing. They remind others that they're not broken—they're becoming.

You can leave your review here:

www.amazon.com/dp/B0F92KQD7X

www.bookbub.com/books/anatomy-of-no-contact-surviving-sile nce-and-reclaimin-your-inner-power-by-sage-charie-monroe

www.goodreads.com/book/show/234373328-anatomy-of-no-con tact

From the quiet ache to the bold return, thank you for walking this pathe with me.

With love,

Sage Charie Monroe

About the Author

Sage Charie Monroe is a writer, storyteller, and advocate for emotional healing and personal empowerment. Her voice is raw, lyrical, and grounded in truth, born from lived experiences, forged through heartbreak, and softened by reflections. Through her work, Sage guides readers on the courageous path of self-discovery, showing that we are never truly alone even in silence.

Behind Sage's poetic presence stands *Dr. Charie Poderoso,* a scholar; educator; and analyst whose decades of academic study and emotional insight form the foundation of every word. She brings clarity and depth to the emotional landscapes Sage explores. Together, these two voices, the analyst and the artist, offer a powerful fusion of wisdom and soul.

This is more than a book. It is a culmination of years of inquiry, resilience, and truth-telling. *Anatomy of No Contact* emerged from heartbreak and silence, a debut that is not just a beginning, but a bold act of reclamation.

Sage's writing reflects both vulnerability and strength. She shares her journey through love, loss, and rediscovery, proving that healing may not be linear but it is alwyas possible.

She lives in Southern California, where she often finds peace in the quiet rhythm of her home. It's there, surrounded by soft ight and the comforting presence of her beloved Goldendoodle, Bailey, that she writes. Whether wandering through nature, journaling, or taking spontaneous road trips, Sage nurtures a life rooted in creativity, presence, and purpose.

You can connect with her at **sagecharie.com** or on social media, where she shares heartfelt insights and tools for emotional healing.

T hank you for walking this road with me. If these words have found a place in your story, I hope they remind you of your own strength and capacity to heal.

May you choose yourself, even on days it feels impossible. May you find peace in your own company. And may you never forget – you are already whole.

With gratitude,
Sage Charie Monroe

www.ingramcontent.com/pod-product-compliance
Lightning Source LLC
Chambersburg PA
CBHW051300120626
46547CB00015B/2029